ON TO THE NEXT THING

a memoir

ON TO THE
NEXT THING

*Believe Every Part of Your Life
Speaks to Unveil Strength and Courage toward Your Destiny*

Marcus Thomas Sr.

Charleston, SC
www.PalmettoPublishing.com

On to the Next Thing
Copyright © 2020 by Marcus Thomas Sr.

Paperback ISBN: 978-1-64990-913-8
eBook: ISBN 978-1-64990-912-1

DEDICATION

Thanks, Dad! Until we meet again.

PREFACE

What just happened to me? I'm sitting here pondering how my life has suddenly changed and I'm thinking to myself, *let's write a book*. This may or may not seem like a normal reaction to any situation in life that may occur for someone else, but my process like always seems to be different yet purposely derived. I was provoked and motivated to share parts of my life and as I embarked on this journey I discovered how much of my life has really mattered. Each one of us has a storied life filled with underlying narrative that guides and also exacts its toll on our very soul. The personal details I share are meant to be a bridge and an invite to anyone willing to explore the deeper meaning of their life and an inspired life map to keep going on to the next thing.

CONTENTS

Chapter 1   The Examination · 1

Chapter 2   Inertia· 13

Chapter 3   Time· 22

Chapter 4   My Inspiration · 33

Chapter 5   What Did You Say? · 46

Chapter 6   Faith Reality· 57

Chapter 7   Change· 68

Chapter 8   Distress and Pain Were Never My Enemies · · · 79

Chapter 9   Tired of Dreaming; Get to Work · · · · · · · · · · · 95

Chapter 10   Success and Benefits on the Inside of Me · · · · 101

Chapter 1

THE EXAMINATION

I t's odd as I sit here. The first thing that comes to my mind is *Marcus how did you get here?* So I started to think to myself, *how about you examine your life to understand some of the details that reveal who you are.* I would hope that, through this perspective, my self-evaluation and detailed inspection would give me insight as to how consistent or inconsistent I have actually been. Counseling, advising, and consoling are some things I've done for others, but now may be a good time to look inward and identify memories, events, flaws, and strengths that have propelled me on to the next thing in my life. For some, this endeavor is suited for a professional or someone with strong wisdom you deeply trust, but I feel like I'm up to the task—since I'm now "unemployed" (not really in love with this term but will get to it later), humbled, and mentally open, as many are when certain streams of life are changed or are cut off from the normal flow.

My parents first came to Chicago in 1970 after leaving Hawkinsville, a small town in the state of Georgia, arriving here with very little. I know this because my parents would share with me and my three siblings when we were young, and this is probably the reason we comprehended thankfulness and appreciation at a young age. But truthfully, the effects of less or just enough, because we were so young, seemed to not impact us. None of our provision was based on what we knew or did. As I think about my parents, I'm trying to imagine how stressful the unknown must have been for them. They packed us and anything they could fit in a car and set out on the eight-hundred-mile path trailing my uncle Willie. I don't remember the ride or the arrival, and as vague as the memories are from that time of my youth, I simply remember having two parents who took care of us, fed us, and made us feel safe. I can imagine that there are single parents who have similar paths and journeys with children and have maintained a sense of family wholeness. But my heart is warmed when I think about the choices my parents made not fully knowing the impact and example they were forging for me and my siblings. To some, they may not be perfect, and by many accounts they may be flawed. But life dealt them a hand, and they didn't sit idle.

My sister is the oldest, then me, with two younger brothers. One was a newborn baby while we traveled here, and the other one came later. I love them all dearly, and you'll hear about them in different parts of this book a little later. I don't want to get into statistics, as that is not my motivation, but I get the sense that parenting is one of the greatest gifts you can give to any child. And it doesn't matter if you're rich or poor; just being there to give your best matters. For every choice or cause you make, there is an effect.

My awareness is heightened at this point, knowing that my childhood was so pivotal and that I would be blessed with not one but two persons to give me a start and help me navigate this life, when this same life was challenging them to restart and figure out this new territory. These two people had the courage to bring me into this world and decided to provide and care for me without asking me what I thought or forewarning me of how frightened they might have actually been. Now before I go further, you might start thinking to yourself, *why would they?* You have to remember as children, we haven't developed the capacity to handle many of life's issues, but we are observant, impressionable, and will eventually have an opinion. The unfortunate truth is that many small children bear the burden of lack and know a level of fear that is reserved for maturity that I to my parents' credit was sheltered from. As I reminisce I'm thankful for two parents and know many have one but I hope and continue to pray that every child can have access to someone with love, patience, and wisdom, to help guide and be an image of perseverance.

When we first arrived in Chicago, we lived with relatives, my uncle and auntie who were my father's brother and sister-in-law. They were established, gracious, and openhearted family who willingly helped my father and mother. There were also other family and great friends who helped give us a terrific start. I have to point out that, amazingly, being with family is probably one of the greatest influences in our cultures, which helps give us a sense of pride and connection, not only in a bloodline but also in rich heritage. Now that I think about it, I better understand the principles of care for others and help and strength through family community, which can dispel and reject the spirit of fear that seeks to, paralyze and offend all of us without warning.

—⟋⟍—

When I was about three years old, I remember waking up in the middle of the night, going to my mom and dad's room, and saying something scratched my toe. My mom half opened her eyes, looked at me, and said, "Go get back in the bed. Nothing scratched your toe." I insisted, so she got up and walked me back to the room, said, "Get back in the bed," then looked at me and asked what I had been doing before this alleged attack. Like any other three-year-old, I said nothing but twirled my feet in the air. I wondered why the frown appeared since it was only about ten thirty at night. Now, keep in mind this was a different era, and my parents believed in having us in the bed by 8:30 p.m., no playing and no noise. But that night I was still kind of wound up and goofing off. All of a sudden, she said that was the devil and "If you don't go to sleep, you're not going to have any toes." I only remember staying still for a few moments and quietly going to sleep.

Why has this memory stuck with me? Is it rudimentary comprehension for instruction and boundaries that, as children, we face and hear in the terms that our young minds can contain? Or simply, at that age, I probably believed my mom was willing to let the devil have my toes if I didn't go to sleep like she said. After that night, I wasn't afraid anymore but had a new awareness of instruction, self-preservation, and careful curiosity. I can only now analyze and describe this event in these terms because it amazes me that as parents, we all look for a way to communicate to our children. That night, I heard my mom clearer than before. It caused me to think before I act (I kept my toes under the cover) and to consider certain possibilities yet do so with healthy caution.

—∿—

I started kindergarten at about age five, and, of course, I'm a little bit older and a little wiser in relative terms. The first week I started, things seemed to be happy and normal considering I was sharing space with about twenty-five other children. Many of us quickly carved out mutual and favored cliques that seemed to help us cope with this new atmosphere and give each of us some sense of security. Group bathroom time was usually a time to get away and to clown around with some of my new friends until we heard the teacher's voice screaming "Let's go!" Why my kindergarten memory centers on the bathroom is strange, but it's another turning point in my life, so stick with me as I recall these different events.

As I settled into routine and things seemed to be going well, in my young mind, I didn't think that at some point, individually, my body would convince me that *there's a task that needs your immediate attention. And go quickly.* This is something I've done at home many times, but I never had to tell the teacher, "It's an emergency. Can I go to the bathroom?"

I don't know how I came to the conclusion as to what an emergency was, but I can say, after hurrying across the hallway, my small body seemed to be performing its own fire drill. As I sat there, the storm began to pass, and I was ready to perform the prescribed practice of rolling toilet paper off to do what we all have been taught to do, carefully and with as much skill as possible.

Shockingly the dispenser was working against me and would not allow more than torn little pieces. I began to become unraveled.

The stall was the largest and most terrifying place I could be and, because I could not finish the task at hand, seemed to have no escape. All of a sudden, I bellowed out, "Somebody, please help me!" over and over again without any response, or so I thought since time had escaped me in my panic.

My teacher finally responded by opening the stall and asking, "What's wrong?" I explained the tissue would not come out for me. She simply began to pull down and out, very slowly, and tissue began to flow out of the dispenser. *Hallelujah!*

After her calm instruction, she said to me, "Now, you finish, wash your hands, and hurry up." That day, I learned things out of your control, even when they appear to be terrifying, ultimately require calm and patience and that even embarrassment can yield positive results.

—⁓—

Fast-forward to third grade when I had seemingly come into my own. Between eight and nine years of age was a decent place to be in. I had my own mind and didn't want to follow anyone except for the girl I was now infatuated with. Her opinion of me was important since I was under some type of stupid spell.

It was late spring, and my class had an opportunity to go outside for recess. During this time, the girls could jump rope, and the guys could play athletic games. Needless to say, while playing baseball, I had to show this particular girl how grand I could be. Not knowing that another guy my age had the same thing in mind, things quickly escalated into a rivalry for her attention. This did not sit well with me since I just knew, at this age, this was the only girl for me in the entire world.

After recess, agitation would linger on throughout the afternoon, and finally at bathroom break, we would settle on whom she liked the most. We got into a bit of a tussle for which I was the victor, but somehow I felt sad on the inside. My actions did nothing to neither impress her nor help my cause in being friends with the guys I had hung out with all school year. I quickly learned that actions leave an impression whether positive or negative, and that impression has an impact on how one may respond to you directly or indirectly. Consideration for others' feelings, along with some degree of self-control, had wiggled its way into my life and would set the stage for my journey in adolescence through preteen years.

—⚉—

In 1977, my parents bought a home on the south side of Chicago. This meant moving away from old friends, surroundings, habits, and any identity of coolness I had established. The day we moved in, I met one of my childhood friends, whose name was Starsky. That wasn't his real name, but during that era, we still had the residue of the show *Starsky & Hutch*. And if you know anything about the show, Starsky was considered the cool one.

I have a lot of great childhood friends who have left me with some of the best memories and have impacted my life. I mentioned Starsky at this point in the examination because the first thing he said to me after we exchanged names was "You got a girlfriend?" We laughed, but I understood that he was the established ladies' man on the block and to stick with him. I of course, considered myself to be more aware in the "I like a girl" syndrome, and after having dealt with my previous experience I understood the power of girls and from then on would proceed with caution.

My mother enrolled us in Foster Park Elementary School. It was down the street from the home we had moved in over the summer. It made way for new friends and new experiences for me and my siblings. Niecy was my big sister. Others had a big brother; I had a big sister. She was strong and self-sufficient and could be rough around the edges and made the guys think twice before approaching. She led the way in gaining the trust and limited responsibility that my parents began to meter out as we entered certain age groups. She would go on through grammar school and then to high school leaving me to navigate grammar school by myself.

Things were going well; I made new friends, created bonds, and even had fun while moving from one grade level to the next. I wasn't an Einstein but always had good rapport with my teachers, as my parents wouldn't have it any other way. They were old-school and did not tolerate disrespect of any kind in or out of the home.

I finally made it to the seventh grade, with Mrs. Thomas. Yes, she had the same surname as me but no relation. She was who everybody warned me about because she had a paddle for unruly students and could be tough if she caught you acting up. Because she frightened me and reminded me of my mother, I focused on my studies with a passion. Things went well leading to something surprising.

Around March or April, she met with my parents and told them it was possible for me to graduate into high school early from the seventh grade if I wanted to. This strange development was unexpected and a product of simply trying to stay on the good side of Mrs. Thomas through studying, acing tests, and earning extra credit, solely to have her tell my parents something positive at teacher-parent conference. This turned into a dilemma since what I thought would be a decision made by the two people who were raising me turned into them asking me, "What do you think? Do you think you can do it?" Suddenly at thirteen, I was faced with choosing to get ready for the next level of education, which I had only talked about with my classmates in future tense, as well as in brief conversations with my sister about how much harder but also fun it was. I threw fear down and walked over it, but all the while, I kept saying to myself, *this is going to be bad if you fail.* Fortunately, I successfully met the requirements, and then headed for promotion.

Graduation came and went, and then summer break arrived. I spent a good part of it thinking about the unknown. Was this how my parents felt at times? There was no turning back. They did ask, "Do you think you can do it?" I started to understand that hard work ultimately gets rewarded and that people watch your efforts even when you don't think so. Thinking back, I had two voices in my head. One was the fearful kid who kept saying, "Don't do that again—it draws too much attention." The other was the strength of my parents saying, "Just keep going—you're going to be all right."

—◊—

My mom was able to enroll me into Simeon Vocational High School in 1981 with the help of Rev. Martin, who was a neighbor and well known for being a tremendous help in the surrounding community. Things went really quick. I went to freshman orientation in August but don't remember anything about the day. I think terror overwhelmed to the point of no recollection of that day even right now.

I was only thirteen but got information and advice from two of my upper-class neighbors who were already at my high school. Our moms knew each other and had suggested that I stick with them to get to know the bus route and overall logistics of high school. They gave me clear instruction on amounts, bus transfer, and most of all, "Be cool," especially arriving in front of the school as a freshman.

On the first day of school, however, I got on the first bus and forgot to get a paper transfer to present to the bus driver on the changeover.

The next driver said, "No transfer, you got to pay."

I ended up asking a bus full of high school classmates if they had change for a dollar, which held up the ride for about five of the longest minutes of my life, before someone took pity and bailed me out, "*thank you but, strike one*," as everyone watched me walk to my seat in freshman shame.

As we arrived at school, I collected myself and said, "*OK, be cool.*" But because of my hold up, timing was a little thrown off. We had discussed getting inside the school early enough to be sociable and not worry about the first bell, which meant you only had a few minutes to get to your homeroom for the first day. But because of me, the plan was to pick up the pace a bit when we get off the bus in order to get ahead of the crowd that would form as they checked for ID.

The pace increased to a small trot, which was no problem until I tripped and slid chest first. I quickly got up as I heard snickers and knew for certain any cool points I had were gone for a good while.

I somehow recovered from the humiliating first day and relatively cruised through my freshman year. I carry this thought with me because I learned firsthand that some days—even with good preparation, instruction, and good intentions—you may miss something, take a fall, or even feel humiliated.

I'm amazed and caught off guard revisiting these few moments that have stayed closest to my heart. We keep fond memories to ourselves and proudly repeat them because they make us feel good. There is nothing wrong with submitting to those truths; they just don't reveal the full capacity of every impression, idea, or character-building network of our life legacy. We block out bad days because they don't fit the narrative described to you that you should ascribe to, but I know that it was me those days. I own it. These events and times in my life may seem so small. But reflecting on the path of my parents and allowing myself to closely think about family input and these odd instances that have stuck with me have helped me realize I am the outcome of condition and circumstance. But the narrative is controlled by me; my response to situations and circumstances are what define who I am. I am a real-life manifestation of my response to everything that God has allowed to come my way. My scale is small and may pale in comparison to someone with more challenging and perhaps harsher experiences. But your response is greater than any temporary circumstance or situation you may find yourself in. Even if you didn't start out with good support or simple help, you are still unique, and it is not too late to respond with the strength of a new and greater narrative.

Chapter 2

INERTIA

Is it me, or does it seem like, at certain times in life, you're walking uphill, or you're driving on the highway in a car that has problems and will barely go the minimum speed? I concede that I might be the only one, but for me, motivation and energy to know exactly what I should do with my life didn't seem to unfold or show up at the perfect or most optimal time as I started to face life as a young adult. The advice, signs, encouragement, and decent direction were all there glaring in front of me, but the will to move swiftly or even have a consistent pace didn't seem to unfold. Time and decisions seem to run together when you know you need to do something, but the rational order and sequence that take advantage of the time you are about to invest seem to walk away and say, "*Catch up, please.*"

I entered a business college after graduating from high school, probably was because my sister was at that same college, or maybe it's because of the pressure you feel in your senior year of high school when teachers, counselors, family, and friends are all asking what you are going to do when you graduate, where you are going to college. I didn't have a clue, and old-school parents would tell you that you got to get a job or go to school. The pressure and expectations were all there, and for a seventeen-year-old going on eighteen, my mind and body didn't seem to have a link for the momentum that was required. I was listening to everyone who had good advice and great ideas, but hearing them just didn't seem to compute. They say when you can actually hear, there is an acute level of attention to detail followed by comprehension and action. I watched others gather up a full head of steam and take off; I mimicked them but didn't have the same drive as they did. So here I am in business school to become a travel agent. That's right. I said, "a travel agent." It's kind of cringe worthy, and a feeling of sluggishness wants to come over me when I think about it. Now, don't get me wrong; there's nothing wrong with being a travel agent or owning your own travel agency. I'm just trying to explain how I tossed myself into this arena.

It lasted for two semesters, and I just lost interest. I didn't have the strength or the fortitude to keep going and finish. This is not how I envisioned things going, yet it felt like the bus was leaving the station, and I was looking at it drive away, saying to myself I should have been on it.

Have you ever heard someone say, "You better get it together; this is your life; time is not waiting on you"? It becomes a common theme when it starts to look like you really don't have a clue as to what you are actually doing. Every now and then, it feels like you get a spark to move or that destiny is calling you, and you know exactly what you're going to do. But all of a sudden, the energy runs away from you, and you're left with that feeling of *you got to figure this out*. So you hit the restart button and draw on resources, thoughts, and ideas that can propel you into the right place and atmosphere that'll get this train rolling.

For me, it was enrolling in junior college and majoring in industrial engineering with an eye on designing bridges and highways. I majored in machine drafting and architecture in high school, so this had to be my light bulb minute. Yelp this was it. I thought I finally found the direction I should be headed in, and surely my energy and heart would kick in and do for me what others were doing all around me.

I enrolled, got my classes, and started showing up, and for one week straight, I was on time and ready to work like never before. Tell me why this momentum acted as if it didn't like me or want to be my friend anymore. Or at least, that was the cartoon that was playing in my head. Why, oh why was this happening to me? I was late for my first class, and the professor would say, "Just get here. Let me help you get through this." But no, I kept digging the hole deeper and deeper, along with neglecting other responsibilities that I was supposed to tend to in the financial aid office.

I barely made it through the first semester, and because of my lethargic ways, I started the second semester but got pulled out a class because I had not secured funding. I somehow crawled through another semester, yet responsible habits just didn't seem to stick to me. And yes, you guessed it. I dropped out, and there I was with a little over one and a half years of college experience but nothing to show for it but student loans.

Starting life without a real passion for something or without having passions turn into real-life accomplishment is like kryptonite that is designed to destroy you or, at the very least, crush your morale. For me, the seeming lack of movement didn't stop me from dreaming. Through all of the negative energy that I was allowing, I kept trying to find the next thing that was right for me. Was it for me to keep trying to finish college at this stage in my life, or should I take a break? In hindsight, I should've kept going and pulled myself out of whatever funk I was in. I opted to take a break and anyone who can relate to having limited work and college experience knows that this background leads to an interesting job path.

I was able to get a job at a day care center, which was sort of fun except for, you know, the work part. This required that I be responsible for children and lesson plans for day care–level students. The experience was one I'll never forget, especially the people. The director was a wonderful lady who was well educated, smart, and no-nonsense, but she was an encourager when it came to education. Not to mention, I was surrounded by women who were strong, highly opinionated, and full of aspiration. Most of them had their degree in childcare; the others were working toward attaining their degree in teaching or other social areas. Somehow it was good for me to be around them as it brought me to the next level of maturity. I'm not sure what happened, but mentally I thought clearer. I gained energy to follow through with tasks, and more importantly, I could hear when one of them would say, "Marcus, what are you going to do about school?" or "What are your next steps toward your goals?"

I can remember conversations but never was offended; felt attacked, or believed they were trying to pry into my business. I had a strong sense that they cared about me, my well-being, and my future as a young man. I'm not saying that I pieced it all together at once, but for me, those small steps were huge in helping me put my feet back on solid ground, so to speak.

—⚏—

I gained more drive and care for the decisions and choices I would make but still didn't have that fulfillment of complete passion. I was helping to mold young minds—talk about irony—while still on my own slow, developing path. Things were a lot better, but I still had that feeling of change needing to happen. This time I could hear better. It wasn't just the faculty that surrounded me; I started to notice and have interaction with young fathers and mothers as they would drop their young children off at the day care center. The conversations, comments, and even the jokes about life would speak to me. Everything had something to do with a certain issue or circumstance that required a certain response, and many things, through inner reflection, allowed me to draw from them. I should probably clarify that the majority of them were young, up-and-coming professionals, and that's not to say I didn't learn anything from other neighborhood parents. I would just notice anyone who seemed to be on that path that I was so interested in being on.

My desire to motivate myself began to grow more and more, and in just a few months, I was, at the very least, a functioning young adult. A few more months passed as I got used to getting a paycheck. Children were calling me Mr. Thomas. I could go back home to my parents' house at the end of the day and have a conversation with some sense of pride, probably because I better understood responsibility is not a suggestion. They didn't feel that way because they believed that my capacity was greater, but I knew deep down on the inside I had to do better.

As I started to allow positive influence, stability, and good patterns to soak into my life, moving with purpose became a lot easier. At times, I would get down on myself and say, "Where was this energy when I first got out of high school?" or "Why did the universe throw molasses in my pathway?" I kept moving, and truthfully I hadn't lost that much time. It just felt like I had wasted an important part of my life. I know I graduated from high school early, but I can't use that as an excuse for my choices and response for a life I'm in charge of.

At eighteen, going on nineteen, I had thoughts of going back to college, but also met a young lady who would be the love of my life, in my sites and on my mind. I assure you that she did not change my mind about school, and as a matter of fact, she was strong, independent, and smart and had the same aspirations about finishing college.

When someone tells you that you are a young adult, I think it's meant to not only prepare you but give you insight into certain freedoms. But what we don't comprehend is that those freedoms come at a cost and require engaged responsibility. For many, if you're like me, it wasn't the fear that captivated me. I believe it was the over thinking, the looking too far ahead, when I should've simply put one foot in front of the other and slowly repeated the pattern until the precision that comes in time allows for a faster pace. When we're young, our parents are constantly giving instruction and guiding because they know what we should be doing next. Maybe I psychologically got used to a pattern, and rightly so. But that pattern helped me to believe I was a self-thinker, a self-starter, and oftentimes I thought I knew it all, when all along I had help in synchronizing my life.

When training wheels come off, that person behind you will all of a sudden let go even when you're not expecting it. They know you can do it, but somehow we lose focus, turn around, and start looking for help that makes you comfortable. When I was learning to ride a bike, I remember, even though the person let go, I found a way to grab a fence with one hand, pedal, and hold the bike with the other. This was a slow pace and really wasn't riding at all. But until I got up enough courage to let the fence go and start riding, then and only then could I learn to trust going faster and turn without falling.

More often than not, it will probably be easy to give up and come away with a self-prescribed notion that something was really hard and difficult, to the point we believe that thing is the problem—when really it is the thing that we don't know that makes it seem hard, difficult, mind-boggling, and a drag. The answers usually stare us in the face. They have all the signs and warnings, blinking and glaring at us, begging for us to pay attention. But I had to ask myself the same question that you may be thinking of, and that is "Aren't there some things that are truly hard in life?"

My experience taught me to say no, and here's why: when you encounter something that you know nothing about, it will seem larger-than-life and have you believe that it is insurmountable. Here's the key: you know nothing about the thing; you have no relationship with the thing; and its sole purpose is not to keep you from knowing about it but to remain true to its purpose. The moment knowledge and light enter in; your relationship with that thing immediately changes. The very thing that we thought was hard has become clearer and accessible and ignites passion.

The most amazing thing is that each part of our life gives us these very same answers. Think about it. When you see a baby, there's a glare in its eyes as it watches you walk back and forth. The baby may whine for you to take him or her up because they want to move like you. But as knowledge unfolds, they learn how to crawl and get from place to place at a slower pace. Then they desire to move faster but have no knowledge until you hold their hand and show them how to walk. This may take a while, and some babies will even take their hand away from your hand because they believe they can do it and have seen you do it many times. But as soon as you let go, they get excited and move too fast and stumble. This is only a temporary setback. We all know through experience they go on with patience and learn to do many things as knowledge increases.

This pattern of gaining knowledge and overcoming obstacles is something that is innate to all of us in various forms no matter what your background or where you come from. The experiences that we all face in these dirt bodies may be unique, and there will be a lot of things, affecting some more than others that seemingly slow or just don't move your way. This is temporary, and you cannot allow it to change your destiny. I believe your impact and legacy in this life are important and greatly matter. Because you're reading this, I guarantee that you have the courage and the strength to get through lack of motivation, inactivity, apprehension and nondirectional behavior, just keep going.

Chapter 3

TIME

When I was a child, things seemed to move at a slower pace, and I thought I had all the time in the world. I am nineteen, a registered voter, and yes, I was already registered with selective services, but somehow it didn't feel like I was a lawful young adult. As I stated, I'm working, being responsible, and have a fairly good command on my life. I seem to have acquired a rhythm for important matters, details, and appropriate actions at the right time without any reminding. I finally had things going in the right direction at that moment and could see the person in the mirror a bit clearer, and oddly that baby face was still staring back at me. I'm laughing because I thought time was supposed to bring about change in appearance, but not for me. I still looked like a little boy—and still no facial hair. My uncle, Eddie Lee, would tease me all the time, saying, "Are you ever going to stop looking like a little boy?"

It just didn't seem right that my younger brother Tony had facial hair at about fourteen, and my dad was showing him how to shave at about fifteen. I just kind of rolled with it, especially since Tony and I were daredevil buddies. We weren't twins, but my mom would dress us alike, and we would always find a way to get in trouble together. From riding Big Wheels at full speed, pretending as if we were going to run someone over but swerving at the last minute, to tightrope walking over boards with nails in them, it was always full speed and think later. I was slim, and he was husky. We went from having Afros to "Jheri curls"—what a mess. We were always close, and it has never changed. But it would've been nice if he would have shared some of that facial hair with me so that my uncle and everyone else around me would have stopped saying I looked like a little boy.

Time is the one thing that we can never get back. It keeps moving forward and never waits. I sang in the choir at my home church and would direct the choir and lead a song every now and then. There was a family group called the Booth Singers who would come to our church and sing for different programs. I knew their brother Greg, who was one of our musicians, and his sister who was married to the minister of music, who was also my older god brother. The entire family could sing, but one sister in particular, named Alice, caught my eye, but I would never say anything. We were getting ready for a spring musical, and my god brother asked the family to join in with us. I only made passing inquiries and comments, but somehow Greg devised a plan where he said, "My sister Alice wants you to come pick her up for rehearsal." This was unexpected but welcome news.

—m—

I got to their home. Greg came out and said, "Here they come."

I wondered, they? But where is your sister.

A group came out, including Alice, but she proceeded to head to the vehicle with her brother, Greg. He looked at her and said, "You can ride with Marcus."

She looked totally unaware of any arrangement, especially one that she initiated.

Greg smiled. I smiled. But she didn't, so the only thing I could think to say was "its fine. You can ride with me. I don't mind."

I had been duped, albeit for good reason. The fifteen-minute ride to choir rehearsal felt like an eternity of awkwardness. Brief conversation followed by quietness seemed to go on forever.

I finally said, while driving, "I'm sorry. I thought Greg said you needed a ride because he had somewhere else to go before he got to rehearsal."

We both smiled as she replied, "No, I didn't tell him that, and I'm going to get him when we get back home." The encounter had the makings of a disaster but turned into something harmless and life-changing all at the same time.

The program came and went, but during the period of about two months, we became good friends and would have great conversations on the phone. We would talk at length about our parents, common upbringing, present and future desires and goals.

About a month into our close friendship, she had shared with me that, at that particular time, she was not looking for any type of serious relationship, and we both agreed that we liked hanging out together and talking. Things were going well. We were growing closer and closer together the more we talked and hung out.

She had a young son, and oftentimes he would go out with us. He would talk and give me all kinds of details about his mom leading to hysterical laughter. These two people appeared in my life, and I really believe I was better for it. The situation and opportunity was perfect for me at that time in my life.

June came, and it seemed as if time walked ahead of me, and I just started to follow. It wasn't a bad thing since I had settled into maturity, but the events that were unfolding had a comfort and unique purpose.

We were standing outside after church one Sunday, and I said, "Come on. Let's go to Giordano's pizza place."

She looked at me and said, "Hey, you can't boss me around. You never even asked me to be your lady."

Inwardly, the stupid in me started to think back to the "Let's just friends" conversation, but the smart me in this paradox stood up and ask, "Would you please be my lady because I am crazy about you?"

We continued on dating and having fun only to look up and find that we had fallen in love with each other. Yelp, I was in love with a pretty girl, and I liked it! I was not planning this, but I was happy and clearheaded without doubt and fear in this relationship.

I have to mention, as odd as it may seem, that age never really came up in the relationship. Don't get me wrong; we both were sure we were of legal age. But the conversation came up about birthdays in September or October, and she asks, "How old are you?"

"Nineteen."

"No, you're not. Let me see your license."

I laughed, reaching, and said, "See."

She smiled and said, "I'm twenty-two,

But I thought you were older than me because you act and talk like a settled older man who looks really young."

The good news is, after a few, you got schooled jokes. We continued on, even to the point of future marriage conversations.

—⁓—

I knew what I wanted and started to think about the avenues for achieving these goals that now included a family.

As I stated earlier, I was active in church and, like many, grew up in the same church culture. I'm going to talk about my faith later but thought it important to bring up a few details for context in the next events in time.

I grew up with a strong sense of moral uprightness, according to God's will for our life, and I won't try to make excuses. I'll simply say that even when we are not faithful to His will, He will consistently love us, but it does not change the requirement for us to be faithful in our commitment and to know that, ultimately, His way keeps us safe, whole, and peaceful and benefits our life beyond measure.

Please understand I know this is personal to me but thought it important to mention for some who might have seen this same path.

That being said, my life was about to take off, and the only thing I thought to do was to buckle up like my parents and move forward.

In December of 1987, we found out that Alice was pregnant, with a due date of sometime in the following September. This would, to say the least, be unknown territory for me, especially since I had not long ago begun to piece my life together. Yet here I was about to take a wife, son, and a new baby.

Time is measured as seconds, minutes, hours, days, and years; relatively, we know it as past, present, and future. For a moment, I felt like all of those elements stood before me and asked, "What are you going to do? Are you ready?"

What I knew for sure, without any doubt, was I was not going to let the person I loved feel one ounce of worry and that we were not letting fear dictate to us for what was to come. As soon as Alice looked at me and asked, "What are we going to do?" I simply said, "We are going to get married and raise our family."

I wanted to make sure I did all I could to let our parents know that I was serious and would not disappoint. So I started with my parents, knowing that they would have some reservations. But this is what I was headed for, and I wanted their blessing.

They were quiet when I started the conversation and just sat, listening, probably in shock since this was not what they saw so soon in my life. As you can imagine, my age was a topic: "Do you understand the magnitude of this decision? And is this truly what you want?"

I could see the worry in my mother's eyes and the wrinkles in my dad's forehead. They didn't realize that, as they were talking, I was staring at them remembering everything they had taught me, every story they had shared, and all that I could remember about the path they took in spite of the obstacles. They were my heroes and the reason why I knew I had the capacity to go this direction. So I looked at them and said, as humbly as I could, that I had prayed like I was taught, and the Lord had assured me that He would help me take care of my family. They knew and loved Alice already. She had been to dinner at the house many times, along with other family functions.

They then responded, "OK, just be sure. We are here for you. But make sure to talk to Alice's parents."

Whew! Mission accomplished.

The next day, I asked Alice if I could talk to her parents. She said, "OK. Let's do it after we get off work tomorrow."

Alice's dad was one of the nicest men I had ever met, and I had a ton of respect for him. Her mom was sweet and stern and was the unknown factor in such a serious matter concerning her daughter and current grandson.

I sat down and began to tell them that I wanted to marry Alice because I loved her and Tarail. I told them I had talked to my parents already and that they had given their blessing.

"I want to make sure I get your blessing before I move forward."

They expressed their desire for the treatment for their daughter and said, "We trust you to do what you said."

—⚊—

We were getting married. That's right. The season of "I" had turned into "we." So we set a date of June 4, 1988. Planning seemed easy to me, but the bride seemed to find herself in different areas of frustration, from wedding-party commitment to everything costing more than we thought. Even though things were coming fast and a small amount of fear hovered around us, we kept focus and assured each other that things were going to work out for our good. All the planning, rehearsals, and fittings were done. The day was finally here. We got married, took a ton of pictures, and had fun with our family and friends at the reception. It was a special day. I have to mention my aunt Mattie, who has transitioned from this life. She volunteered to go to the reception hall to receive delivery of the wedding cake, which meant she couldn't be at the church for the wedding. She was a huge part of my life, from helping to see after me and my siblings to memorable family dinners at her home. Her love and care meant the world to me and Alice. There are pertinent periods in life that have meaningful impact; her willingness to go and wait for our cake was a perfect example of love in action that I will never forget.

The day was special and complete, but we were beat. The congratulations, wish-you-wells, and private marital advice sessions were all received in good faith. But after the honeymoon, we had to get to our life.

We had our new apartment lined up, and a couple of days later, we were moving our stuff away from our parents' homes. The first night at our new place Alice went right to sleep, I was up late thinking and planning. I would be lying if I said a shadow of fear did not come over me, but all I thought to do was tell myself, "It's time. You can't give any of your time to fear.

Was there a manual for a twenty-year-old to guarantee continued progress or ensure how the next sequences of events yield success? I was past those feelings of *I don't know what to do next*; I was ready to fight for my family. I had made promises to my parents and Alice's parents that I was not going to fail at. I understood the purpose of dreams and the benefits they offer, they give you hope with anticipation for great potential. But I focused on promises.

For anyone who faces life and its unknowns, know that promises are made of words and that words impact time. The impact of words in time is a provision that is attached to every promise, and I believe that when a promise is made, time carries those words with the expected end. This does not absolve us of our responsibility to make wise decisions or from the possibility of making mistakes, but keeping or neglecting your word reveals who we are in time.

I knew that Alice and I were young with a tailor-made family, but I had strong feeling that we could succeed. We often take time for granted, missing out on opportunities that are found in certain seasons and periods that I believe are ordained by God. The questions that often appear are, did I move to soon? Did I correctly calculate the enormity of what's required? And do I have enough patience to stay focused on the present, forget the past, and let my future be governed by sound judgment and promises.

Time doesn't yield. It simply wants to be respected as our vehicle that's willing to reveal our potential, growth, relationships, recovery from mistakes, comfort from pain, and definitely the expectation God has placed in each one of us. This may sound like nonsense to some, but recounting this journey I was about to embark on brought all of this to remembrance in a more unique way for me. Whether teachings from my parents or life encounters, I knew these things and wisdoms that were driving me, but with better understanding and patience translated by time.

When you're as young as I was, and perhaps many can relate, you don't fully articulate every part of your life in total understanding. But in spite of varying obstacles, I still believe our capacity is greater than we can imagine.

Here is how I started to move subconsciously in time with just hope and faith. I couldn't let life paralyze me. I was married with a family, like my parents, so I had to believe that despite my background or past, potential was still rooting for me to move forward. And so can you.

Growth does its best to help us measure our actions by reminding us that better days and increase belong to us. Our relationships—no matter the degree of connection, whether temporary or permanent—take time from your life. Make them count by listening to the information, whether spoken or shown. They will leave an impression on you, but you are in control of the narrative. When we make mistakes, if we own up to them internally first and become teachable, time will help lead us to corrective actions that can redeem what may have been misplaced or lost.

Most of us will choose comfort over pain. But at some point in time this life will bring an experience of pain that wants to take time from you. The authority to overcome still belongs to you; just keep moving forward during those times.

As a young man I probably couldn't explain the way I'm explaining now, but every inch of me wanted then what I'm now expressing and to succeed. We draw on so many influences, words, and experiences that can be accessed at points in our life and in times of spiritual reflection. The truth is that the image of good and triumph rest deep inside us ready to teach us how to progressively endure. We have to practice not letting the cares of life distract us from the times of our relevant present and the future of great expectation. If we are willing to practice, our good practice will hopefully turn into good habits, and our good habits become a time of mastering.

Chapter 4

MY INSPIRATION

The thoughts, ideas, concepts, plans, suggestions, mental construct, and knowledge we gain are all caused or encouraged by something or someone. Often these things and people stick with us, leaving an image and intersecting our nerve center pathways, causing us to think and move.

I had seen and experienced a few things that impacted my life to the point where I had formed an opinion about certain things, marriage being one of them. I knew how I wanted to be married, and I stayed grounded in the things I said to myself about marriage. I saw my parents navigate through together, but I also saw other couples who I admired from a distance.

Growing up, my family mingled with other families to the point that it seemed as if we were a part of that family. One of the couples in that family, Jimmy and Marguerite, seemed to be one of the coolest and fun-loving couples I can remember seeing as a young boy, not that that's the only thing marriage is about. They just seemed to get along well and have fun all at the same time, even while raising children and working jobs. Just from my viewpoint, the things

I saw in them were what I wanted when I got married. I understood that it would take more than just having fun or being cool. But it felt good to know that you could meet someone and expect to spend your life together and enjoy it like you're the best of friends on a long, exciting adventure. Alice and I talked about all of those things and were committed to that attitude toward one another.

It had only been two months since we had been married, and things were well. You might say, "It's only been two months," but we felt like we had a handle on this area. Alice was only a couple of weeks from the due date and looked every bit of "Please, let this be over." She was ready and even had a false alarm in which she got rushed to the hospital by my speed demon brother, while I was at work, only to be told, "Not yet." It's interesting as I think about it, and I'll probably have to tiptoe on this subject about how men aren't designed to carry a baby for nine months. But watching Alice carry our son all those months made me realize that women have an extraordinary sense of patience, and in my humble opinion, that is more than likely the reason they make us wait on them as they figure out what to wear.

My mom advised me and insisted that while your wife is pregnant, you make sure she is dressed well and that her hair is done. I tried my best to oblige and pay attention just like my mom insisted, but it wasn't hard. Alice was beautiful while she was pregnant, like so many other women. Her skin was so smooth. To see her carrying my child was an amazing thing. We knew a boy was coming; the only thing we prayed for was that he be healthy. It felt almost perfect knowing that we would have two boys, and, ironically, we had talked about that scenario in our perfect family construct. But life can throw curveballs that will challenge your thinking and humble your heart.

The time had finally come, and we were at the hospital waiting for the doctor to say, "It's time to push." And of course, I was smiling and proud of this glorious occasion in which I would become a father. Alice, however, was uncomfortable, tired, and restless.

The doctor came in, checked her, and said, "It's time."

I smiled and said, "OK, here we go."

She looked at me. No smile.

It seemed like in a matter of minutes the room got crowded, and things started moving fast. After a few minutes and a few pushes, out came my baby boy. Of course, I was excited, made noise, and was happy to cut the cord. I was talking to Alice in excitement, still no smile from her, and asked the doctor and nurse, "Is everything OK with my boy?" I was so excited, and the noise sort of lingered on for a few minutes. But that curveball just had to show up.

A nurse came in our room and gently placed her hand on my shoulder and said, "Congratulations, but can I ask, if you don't mind, lowering your voice?" I smiled because I knew I was loud, but what she said next has stayed with me. She proceeded to explain that directly next door was a mom and dad who were experiencing the pain of their stillborn child simultaneously to our birth. She said that they were taking it really hard but could hear the joy next door. My heart sank at that moment; I instantly felt their grief and replied yes to her request. I could only imagine the pain they were feeling, and the only thing I knew to do was silently pray for them.

I was happy for the birth of our son but became humbled and grateful. That day taught me not to take any part of life for granted. We move and act sometimes without regard for the plight of others, but that day gave me a passion for consideration of others. It's not that we should not have been happy. But for me, my capacity for joy and compassion greatly increased to the point of better understanding for the varying spectrums of life that all of us experience at any given time. I'm not trying to simplify the pain life can bring, and my analogy of the curveball was only to show how sometimes life can feel like you're swinging and missing. But I pray passionately, daily, that whenever pain shows up, not just for me but for everyone, your joy comes one hundredfold.

I wanted to be the best husband and father that I could be even though my execution was based solely on ideas of young understanding and trickled-down comprehension. I had been married for a little over a year, and at that point, I had submitted to focusing primarily on my wife and family. For me, this meant doing whatever needed to be done, even if I violated the old-fashioned-man code of who does what in the home. Both Alice and I grew up in homes where our mothers shouldered most of the household duties, while our dads went out in the labor force. I don't think we were in-fluenced by changed times; I think we just simply would do whatever needed to be done that better suited our household.

I knew upfront, when we first met, that Alice had lim-ited cooking skills, so doing most of the cooking was not a problem for me. We both worked full-time with different shifts. She worked 8:30 a.m. to 5:00 p.m., and I worked 3:00 p.m. to 11:00 p.m. Even though the schedules were not the most convenient, we made it work. Having family help was priceless. Everyone does not have access to family, but relations who lend a hand every now and then should be appreciated and never abused.

Our weekdays would start with us getting up early to get Tarail to Alice's mom's house if he hadn't already spent the night. She would take him to school. She could be highly protective of Tarail and, at times, very possessive, and un-derstandably so since she had helped to raise him before we got married. Alice and Tarail had a routine in place already, and I didn't want to overly interfere since all of this was new to him also. Marcus Jr. was still a baby. So after dropping Tarail off if necessary, I would drive Alice to work, then return home with the baby, fix breakfast for us, give him a bath. Then we both would usually drift back off to sleep for a short nap. At about 1:30 p.m., we headed back out the door so that I could drop him off at my mom's house to keep until Alice got off work. When you're young and energetic, "doing and going" are usually never a problem. You figure things out at your level and speeds, then press go.

It seemed as if things would stay a certain way forev-er, but youth is fleeting and arrogant at times because we haven't realized that, despite your best effort, life can and will change. When change comes, it redirects you, and this is small when you are mature or understand a choice has to be made, and life will go on.

We lived in our first apartment for two years, and then, all of a sudden, the landlord decided to raise the rent. This was not in our plan and presented itself when we were comfortable right where we were. Alice and I sat down and talked, then decided not to renew the lease and look for a new apartment. This brought with it a set of new challenges since it seemed as if everything started to increase in cost during the '90s. We had a really nice two-bedroom apartment, and our young minds had our hearts set on equal accommodations. Everything we saw and liked had a higher price demand, but still we pressed on looking for what we desired. We finally set our heart on a garden apartment with a wonderful lady named Mrs. Crockett. The rent rate was perfect for our young family, and the apartment was clean and in really nice shape. But when your mind and heart are singularly focused and excited, you can be caught off guard by varying circumstances.

—m—

The time at the end of our current lease was getting short, so Alice called Mrs. Crockett before she could call us, only to find out that she had chosen someone else. Motivation can be a powerful tool and never causes regret, and at this point in my life, my young family is what I had learned to live for. So we picked ourselves up from the disappointing news and began the intense search again. Alice and I were continually praying for a place that was nice and affordable, but despite our effort, it seemed as if we were going to have to settle for something that wasn't as nice but affordable or something nice and potentially above our comfortable budget level.

As time had just about run out, and we were down to the last thirty days of the lease, we settled for a place that was nice and a bit above our budget. But that was the least of our worries; the landlord of this facility seemed to have a harsh and intense unfriendliness toward people. I can understand that she, as a landlord, might have had some disappointing tenants, but we had not moved into her facility nor ever met her before applying for a place with her. After hearing her extreme list of do's and don'ts, especially with regard to children, and what she would do if we were ever more than three days late with rent, we reluctantly placed a deposit down. We left feeling dejected but resolved to only stay at her property for one year due to time constraints.

It's amazing that disappointment can break you or be an extremely useful tool that causes a higher level of ability to awaken on the inside. We knew this didn't feel like the direction we should be headed in but didn't allow this to become bigger than it was. So we kept praying and asked God to keep us and show us favor in finding the next place after we finished this new lease. For those who may not believe, I can comprehend and ultimately respect your choice. But I love to encourage people to pray and expect results, and can testify that things can turn when you trust God.

We had started packing and preparing ourselves for this next journey and even started joking about our new evil landlord when, all of a sudden, I got a call from my mother at work saying that Mrs. Crockett was trying to reach me or Alice as soon as possible. I called, and Mrs. Crockett explained that the other people wouldn't work out and asked if we had found a place already, and if not, we could rent from her. This was the best day of our young lives, and I began to explain to Mrs. Crockett that we wanted her apartment but had put down a deposit on another place but had not signed the lease. I asked if she would be willing to wait until we got our deposit back, and she simply said yes.

It took a few days and a very uncomfortable conversation with the surly landlord, who decided that she would return our deposit but was keeping fifty dollars for her trouble. We gladly conceded to this peaceful compromise in order to move away from this situation that felt unnecessarily oppressive. And after about a week or two of redirecting, we finally moved to our new place.

The momentum finally seemed to be shifting, and certain things like our earning ability, situational maturity, and smooth household management were all clicking; at least, that's what I perceived. We were living in a home that was rent-friendly and with neighbors who were concerned, helpful, and peaceful. We lived in the garden apartment. Mrs. Crockett and her family lived on the first floor, and Aaron lived on the third floor. It seemed as if all was right in the world. You may be thinking to yourself that something bad was about to happen, but it was quite the opposite.

Alice found out that she was pregnant again, and while this was happy news, it just caught us off guard. Again, this was what was going on in my mind and from my perspective: two boys, no diapers, a peaceful household, and a stable income deserve a "life is good" stamp of approval.

There are some changes that cause you to just settle in and prepare yourself for the next thing to come. This was the case for what was happening in our life at this point. Alice and I had recently moved our membership away from my home church and were attending a new church while going through this pregnancy. I mention this because the influences on my life were not only new but different. The membership was primarily made up of young people with a few elders mixed in, beside the pastor Joe Pitts and his wife, co-pastor Allie Pitts.

Much of their focus was helping young people mature in life and faith. This was perfect for me. It seemed as if I had hit a calm but uncertain plateau in what I thought life should be, but still felt highly motivated. Also it felt nice to be a part of an impactful church assembly who provided stable advice and spiritual encouragement. I also have to note I met my best friends at this assembly, which for me was very rare. I met Tyrone first (didn't really like him), then Lonnie. These two guys were raising their young families just like me and provided a sounding board for marital and family things we had yet to figure out.

As the pregnancy progressed, Alice started to have minor complications with her back and other things, which made us, visit the doctor more often and, consequently, have an early ultrasound. I always wanted a daughter and was hoping for one in the back of my mind but didn't get my hopes up. So sure enough, the person did the ultrasound, and we had to ask if she could tell what we were having.

She said, "It looks like a boy."

I wasn't disappointed but thought to myself, *Oh well, I'll have three boys.*

As time went on, Alice would say, "It feels like a girl."

And of course, I would say, "You might as well get ready to have another knuckleheaded little boy running around."

And she would say, "Good!" since she loved boys.

—⚬—

The months went by, and as Alice got farther along, things felt strange for me, not in the way some may think; I wasn't scared or panicked but more concerned about having three children and all of the provisions that would be needed. It made me introverted and more methodical in my approach to everything, but as you can imagine, it didn't work well for Alice since her hormones were all over the place and everything was achy.

June 1991 came around; Alice was only eight months but had to stop working by doctor's order. We thought she would make it full-term, but this baby had other plans, and Alice really wanted to be done with this pregnancy. I was working at a place called Temple Steel on the night shift and got a call from Alice saying that she was in labor and heading to the hospital.

My manager urged me on "Go! And congratulations in advance!"

Somehow I made it to the hospital before Alice, and I started asking nurses where my wife was at, only to be told, "Maybe you have the wrong hospital." Ten minutes later, they showed up, and off we went to a private room to get set up for the arrival of my new son.

She was having contractions, yet somehow I fell asleep as we had been there for about three hours. She woke me up by yelling, "Are you really asleep? My water just broke."

I moved quickly and told the nurse Alice's water broke. She came in and said, "Let me check," then said, "I'll go get the doctor."

A few minutes later, the room filled with people saying, "It's time." And of course, I was wide awake then. In my mind, I was trying to think of another boy's name but couldn't concentrate with everything that was going on at that moment. Alice started to push and was so tired, but the doctor kept saying, "One more push" And of course, Alice was squeezing the life out of my hand—probably payback for going to sleep.

The next moments were a blur because the doctor uttered something strange. He proclaimed, "She's out," and I mentally dismissed it for a few seconds. He then confidently announced, "Congratulations! You have a girl."

I shouted, "What! It's a girl!" very loudly. The nurses laughed at me, but they didn't understand I was expecting a boy. I looked at Alice and said loudly again, "Baby, it's a girl!"

She looked at me and said, "I told you," then closed her eyes.

After I made sure Alice was OK, I didn't want to let my daughter out of my sight. But of course, they wanted to take her for a full checkup since she was an eight-month baby.

About an hour later, things settled down, and the nurse brought her to me and Alice and asked, "Do you have a name?"

I said, "Yes, I do. Her name is Octavia Marie."

Alice asked, "Where did you get that pretty name from, since we both were supposed to have boy names ready?"

I replied, "When I worked at the day care center years ago, there was a little girl who took to me like a little shadow, and I told her, 'If I ever have a little girl, I am going name her after you.'"

As sure as we live and breathe, there are going to be influences, suggestions, opinions, communications, and, hopefully, tons of positive revelations concerning life. If you lean solely on human perspective, you are always going to get the limits of our human concern, actions, and emotions. This is not to say that it is wasteful or altogether wrong. Looking at these parts of my life, I can truly say that people have been extremely instrumental in my life. But as I write about my life, I truly dig deep, in retrospect of how these things have caused me to be, push, and move by more than just intellect or feeling. There may be some who disagree or simply believe that the human element, our experience, is all that exist. And I am not offended nor want to cause offense. But I am choosing to believe that my family, friends, wife, and children are all part of the blessing and favor that God designed intentionally for me individually—to mold, shape, and inspire me at the most perfect times in my life.

As I think back on the growth of mental capacity, especially when things appeared to be uncertain—the ability to want more, be better, not just for myself but for my family and friends—I see how these divine-sent investments given to me were so precious and deserve a return. You are more than just under circumstances you see; you are blessed with the people around you and the opportunity to be inspired by the times and events taking place in your life.

Chapter 5

WHAT DID YOU SAY?

How often do we pay attention to the words that we say out of our mouth? Do we think before we speak, or do we even comprehend the thoughts and emotions that are about to be vocalized? Do we hear and listen for alertness and to give consideration? It all matters, especially in the atmospheres and environments we have impact on.

Growing up, I was a young man of few words but was stern and direct as to what I wanted and didn't want, while mildly considering others. This worked well for me when I was a single person living at my parents' home with very little responsibility. It turns out that this approach was severely lacking in terms of clear, precise, and fruitful communication when concerning other people and choices. Who would have thought that being married with growing and increasing responsibilities would require me to communicate so many words for what I thought only required a simple yes or no answer? Not to mention that no one told me that this was mandatory, along with trying to filter through and hear words in everyday life that would come faster than I could process.

I might be overstating what it felt like, but after Octavia got here, life sped up a bit. This wasn't horrible; it was just the next dimension of what our family and my perception to life had become. I had a wife and two boys, but now there was another lady in my life who took my brain away, because I adored her. My daughter is not the focus of these revelations, but I mention her and the impact she had on me because it changed me into someone with overly protective sensitivity, which most guys with daughters usually have. I wanted to be the best for my family, but having a daughter seemed to cause the worry demon to periodically sow a seed of fear and panic.

Alice and I talked a lot when we were dating, and when we first got married, I could hear her and understand everything she said. But for some reason, this added responsibility and expanded family required different goals, which I thought would automatically appeal to both of us. So in my mind, the words had already revealed themselves in common knowledge.

We both put immediate family needs first, but somehow we stopped communicating in our finances with regard to our disposable income, which consequently filtered out into having limited basic conversations. We brought in decent money, and, even with Alice on maternity leave, there was a surplus. So I assumed that the unspoken common goal would reflect a pattern of saving and good credit managing. I will say upfront that this was my fault, but at the time, I couldn't see my way to clear communication.

Alice loved to shop for herself and the children. There would be a new bag coming in the door just about every other day. But instead of me sitting down and going into detailed planning, I would shut down, be frustrated, and then watch Alice return the same behavior.

I kept moving and pressing toward normal, and I can't tell you why. Maybe it was my turn for a hormone imbalance, overactive testosterone, or an adverse effect of worrying. But I developed an awkward habit of slowly reacting to hearing good advice that probably would have put me ahead of life's curve. I could hear something that was better for me in the long run, but somehow I would bypass it only to come to an unfavorable outcome that felt like déjà vu. None of it put my family in harm's way, but it didn't aid in best future planning practices either.

My family was young, and we were in a good place, but I knew I needed more for my family. We would often visit my mom and dad on Sunday after church, and my mom would see me with Alice, my boys, and our new baby and look at us with so much pride. It felt really good to know I was making my mom happy, but in the back of mind, I knew she had some additional information to share.

I had heard it before, but she, as a mother, thought it important to keep saying it. She would say, "Marcus, you need to go back to school and finish getting your degree in mechanical drafting." I knew she meant well, but that was the furthest thing from my mind at that time, and I did not want to mess with the current routine. This probably would have expanded my career path and created greater leverage for my future. But I wasn't hearing strategy; I heard, "Blah blah…go back to school."

As I stated before, I worked at Temple Steel, and while working there, they had an entry path for different types of engineers. I knew in my mind that I could do the work if I was given an opportunity, but, you guessed it, you needed a degree. I'm not going to rant about everybody needing college and a degree. This was about me hearing the strategy my mom really believed I was going to need and her insistence that all of her children not miss any good opportunity. It weighed on me for a bit in 1991 because she would have helped with the children if I had pushed to go to school in the morning before work, but I bypassed it and kept on going my way.

—⁓—

The natural assumption is that if you have ears, you can hear, but the audible tones coming in are useless if you're not listening. My dad used to say, "Keep living" and that life can be the best teacher, especially if you are slow to hear and act accordingly. Toward the end of 1991, I was at work and feeling good. I was strong and had been athletic prior to marriage. The guidelines for lifting heavy objects had been communicated as well, as that night the older guys said, "OK, Hercules, don't hurt yourself," but they couldn't have been talking to me. Didn't they see me lifting those steel cages by myself with ease? Well, you guessed it. I picked up the last cage—or let me rephrase—I reached to grab, and everything locked, and I could not move. Coworkers came over to check on me, and my supervisor made arrangements for me to get to the emergency room, but all I could think about in the beginning moments was what the guys who warned me thought about me.

I got a full examination, and the doctor said, "It looks like you tore a muscle." I received a prescription for pain relief and muscle relaxation along with rest for a few weeks. I think the humiliation of "I told you so" bothered me more than injury pain that night, but it also changed the course of my health. Anybody who has ever had a back injury will tell you the back never quite feels the same again.

My brothers, whom I am very close to, came to drive me home that night and give me a bunch of silly wisecracks once they found out I was going to be OK. I laughed with them, but on the inside, I started to wonder about the coming weeks and what I had done to myself. Why didn't I listen? And why did this injury have such a profound impact on my daily functions? I had young children who I was used interacting with and a routine that required movement that had been restricted. This was really inconvenient, and it made me cranky from time to time.

Alice would say, "It will be all right," and she would try to do more, especially with my pay being reduced due to worker's comp. I knew Alice cared and wanted me to take my time, go through physical therapy, and get well, but things just didn't feel the same anymore, not to mention she had developed this habit of telling me to "Be nice." I cannot figure out why, but whenever she would say that, it would cause me to growl, and she would look at me and just laugh while trying to hug me.

Being around the house and not working meant I had to talk. Alice had no problem talking, but I had to get back into that type of rhythm. I didn't think it would be hard because we did a lot of talking while dating, but somewhere along the line, I simply became a problem solver with a pointed arrow. The problem with trying to constantly point and shoot is that it's not always specific or target-driven with complete strategy. If we disagreed, we would just get quiet for days, and then start talking again about other things. I think I had this habit with everyone I talked to, and as long as the words were pointed in the direction I was going, you were in my circle.

I know it sounds funny, and I don't believe I was overly ignorant about it…maybe just a little stupid. There are other words to be heard, and some are not always what you want to hear. You are responsible for listening to have the information necessary to relay appropriate responses. But because I was still in my own way, I consequently was about to receive a crash course in words.

While off work for about six weeks, I got better, and through therapy I learned how to stretch and lift as a way of life with this soft tissue injury. Right around the end of September, I got the OK to go back to work, but being back didn't have the same feeling as before. I moved and worked carefully, not wanting to repeat that type of pain ever again. The weeks began to pass, and the New Year had come. I was back in a rhythm, and the family was doing well. I still had frustrations with our financial arrangements, but we or more accurately I hadn't buckled down and used words to solve the issue.

In the middle of January, we began to hear rumors of a layoff coming on my job, and the uncertainty of who was targeted led to many conversations. Guys were saying so many things, some factual and some from pure speculation, but no one had concrete direction. I had experienced disappointment and even understood the fear that accompanies when the unknown is present. But this was something of greater impact because I had heard the word *layoff* and knew what it meant, but hearing that it may be my fate caused an internal panic. I kept it to myself at the beginning. I didn't want to tell anyone or hear any advice right then. In hindsight some type of dialogue with Alice might have been beneficial; I however did not take that opportunity. I let it keep me up at night, playing the scenarios of my life over and over again, praying that I didn't have to hear or listen to those words.

A couple of weeks passed, and just before our starting time the executive officers called the entire shift to the main conference room. My heart was racing on the inside, and I could hear my mom, my dad, and Alice asking, *what are you going to do now?* Or *How about you try this or that?* The CEO explained the "why" concerning the economy, in grave detail. His words were the only sound in the room and every syllable had weight. The managers began calling names. But to my surprise, my time leveraged me ahead of the cutoff by one person.

A few months went by, and it was now May. The weather was starting to be nice, but the steel industry hadn't gotten much better. This time around, it wasn't just a random rumor; it was my supervisor and some managers telling many of us that they are looking to do another layoff.

It didn't take long. As a matter of fact, just days after the discussion, they started calling people to the office. My supervisor waived for me to come to the office. And trust me; it was the longest walk I had taken to this point in my life. When I went in, my supervisor, along with a manager, said a lot of things, but I can't remember any of it. I did hear those dreaded words: "They're laying you off."

The last thing they said to me was that I needed to go to the personnel office to get some paperwork. When I got there, a few guys were there already, and we just half spoke and said, "This really sucks." I went in, listened to the direction, got my paperwork to file for unemployment, and then proceeded to head home.

While driving home, I rehearsed words to say, but by the time I got there and walked in the house, Alice looked up with surprise and said, "What are you doing home? You don't feel well? Why did you go if you weren't feeling well?"

Somehow, as she went through her scenarios, I was able to put on a half smile and say, "Looks like I'm going to be home for a little while."

She looked at me, and I simply said, "I'll tell you about it later."

She said OK and went back to helping Tarail with his homework.

Wow! Somehow I was able to string together a group of words that would relay brief but detailed enough information, incite comfort, calm fear, and keep peace. I jumped in and started fixing dinner, and I knew she had an idea of what happened. But I wasn't going to let those words make my household sad. We talked after the kids got settled and reassured each other that we got this. I just wanted her to be able to go to sleep and not worry.

—ɯ—

I was on unemployment benefits for a few months, and I hated it. I hated having to go to the office to be treated like I was inconveniencing someone or hearing a condescending voice, and I hated that I had to prove that I was looking for a job. I understood there was fraud, but the notion that it's a general habit, and therefore by default everyone is suspect, leaves a bad taste. Oddly, through this process, my ability to speak, hear, and process at the same time was expanding, and I was becoming more open. We kept things afloat and seemed to be on the same page, not to mention I had a talent for automotive repair and would hustle with minor jobs.

It wasn't long before I got a job at an aluminum extrusion plant. This was a fulfillment of a prophetic word spoken to me by my pastor. I talked about my new church home earlier and bring it up again because of the spiritual help they enriched our lives with. While I was unemployed our pastor would constantly encourage us. This was immensely helpful to us as a young couple who had started to experience the minor mental strains of life. I mentioned the word *prophetic*. That word essentially means "spiritual prediction" or "to understand better," a prediction concerning your life according to what God has said about us in His word, or commonly, the Bible. You can read words like "He promises that you will have victory in hard times" or "We are blessed with everything we need for life." But when my pastor reminded me of what God promises, he said to me, "You're going to receive a job offer this week."

Now, some may say, "You were going to get the job anyway," and I understand those opinions. But 1992 was a year in which the economy wasn't at its best for job search in the blue-collar sector. So when my pastor said it to me, it felt good, but I was focused on the experience I was having and just thought they were encouraging words. It came to pass, just like he said, and I started the job and worked for about three months. Then, you wouldn't believe, I got laid off again.

A few months ago, hearing those words along with the other conversations and forms of unfavorable news would have been a source of frustration, but the encouragement by people with more wisdom than me helped me to hear, listen, and process with patience. This season made me better and more comfortable with change happening to me. I still didn't have my degree, but whenever the conversation would come up, I was open to the idea now that I had time off again.

I had a more strategic focus on finding a job but was also doing volunteer work with the young people at the church. This was one of the most rewarding times of my life, probably because the young people were where I used to be, which made me more conscious of my attitude and ability to inform with words coming out of my mouth.

These are only a few examples from my life that were impactful to me, and within such a short time, I got a crash course in the capacity and power of words. Why should this matter to me? Or why is this wisdom so necessary?

Words matter, and at the very moment you speak them, they spark to life with form, seeking the space they were intended to occupy. The second that they are sown, they cannot be taken back but continue on to their target source looking for a root path. I now understand that there are many different words, some designed to hurt and tear down and others designed to build up, communicate a direction, relay a thought, remind you, or simply give you limits.

When we truly listen to the words and decide to allow them to take root, we are moved and transformed by their impact. Not speaking words can be the same as not hearing. When you don't say what needs to be said, nothing moves, changes, or is known; when you don't hear or comprehend the words, nothing moves, changes, or is known. We will always be surrounded by words as long as we breathe, whether spoken or heard. The hope is that we master the context of thought to speech, and understand that those words are about to shape attitude and environment.

It is also important that we hear and listen with patience. This is probably one of the most cherished lessons of my life. When we listen to comprehend what's being said, it creates a time to gather intent, degree of concern, and varying forms of direction, which can lead to constructive action if we are inclined to its path and journey. Those paths, even when the nature of the words seem to be unfortunate, negative, and mean, can have value and potentially lead to something new or better.

Chapter 6

FAITH REALITY

What is faith? Why does faith matter? How does it benefit me? How do I start? And how do I keep on believing. These were just a few questions that came to mind. If you're like me, you haven't struggled with faith. I simply think I didn't have a complete understanding of who I am and how faiths nature mattered to me.

I spoke briefly about my growing up in church and how active I was as a young man, even to the point that I met my wife in church. It probably will sound like a cliché, but I'll say it anyway. Growing up in church or going to church does not guarantee a path or advantage to wisdom and good sense. Every one of our realities will be based on our perception, experience, and some form of influence. These factors tend to play out in every culture and language. That being said, I can only give you parts of my life that may offer some insight and hopefully something positive that leads to a confirmation of hope and not hindrance.

In 1993, I was still laid off but as happy as I could be. Or let me rephrase that: I had a profound sense of joy. I had often heard my parents say, "You got to trust and believe with a strong conviction."

And like so many others, I too looked and said to myself, "OK, I guess," and blindly accepted it as a good way of looking at life. I won't say things were different, but I will say I was different. I started to study more through Sunday school and through midweek Bible study sessions at our church. Again, I can understand if someone may say they acquired some of the same wisdoms through other teachings, but I hope my version of events and influences are of some benefit.

February of the same year came, and as usual, I would pick up the children in the church van on Saturdays for certain activities. This particular day, one of the kids asked, "What is faith?" But instead of giving a long, customary biblical answer (which references Hebrews 11:1), I felt an urge to explain it to them in a simpler way that they could apply to their young lives. I told them that faith is an ability to believe and that everybody has the ability to believe. To give an example, I related to them how we are all equally created with the same measure of ability, and that you can choose where you extend yourself to grow in what you believe.

While we were having this wonderful conversation, the kids said some of the things that they were going to trust God to help them with. I realized that, hey, I needed to do personally what the kids were doing. They said things about their future and even things that, on the surface, I thought were beyond their comprehension. But so what? They were using their ability to the fullest.

—ᵐ—

I was really ready to go back to work. But this time, I prayed and asked God for a job that would allow me to work a normal nine-to-five to be at home with my family and to be off on weekends and holidays. Some may say that when you really want to work, you will accept the first thing that comes your way. I understand that resolve, so trust me; it was in the back of my mind. But I was going to lay my faith out there and hoped nothing would interfere with what I believed.

This mattered to me and felt like a defining moment for what I would do next with my life. I could take the time out and go back to school to finish my degree, but the timing just didn't seem right at that moment. And I know it sounds like another excuse, but I promise you my heart was for the immediate well-being of my family more than anything.

Alice was working on a job that she did not like, not to mention that we were paying over two hundred dollars biweekly for health insurance through her job. It felt like the best thing that I could do was to really believe that things were going to get better, and this time I wasn't trying to channel my parents or anyone else. These circumstances mattered to me, and from what I was learning and studying, I really believed that God cared about me and my household.

Within that same month, Alice got a new job with slightly better benefits, and things got better. She also found favor with the owners of the company in a very short time because of her work ethic.

I would pick her up from work, and they would wave to me and briefly speak. I was never ashamed of being laid off and used any networking avenue I could. Consequently,

Alice mentioned this to one of the owners in passing and stated that I was looking and had been on the waiting list for the Cook County Sheriff's Office for almost two years. He said that he knew someone and would inquire as to my positioning.

I was excited and hoped that this would work out in my favor. So I waited a couple of weeks, then followed up with Alice but didn't want to put her in an uncomfortable situation with the owners. The end of March was near, and my eligibility for the sheriff's office was about to expire. So Alice made an effort to ask, but the connection didn't come through. I wasn't sad; I knew and believed there had to be something better coming for me.

I worked from time to time doing construction with my play-father, who was my friend Ellis's dad. His dad reminded me of my dad in how diligent they were in making a living for their family. Seeing and working with him made me want good things for my family even more. But I didn't panic; I just kept believing and hoping for something good to emerge.

One of the members at my church was a trustee and a missionary, who I worked with on one of our youth projects. Betty Davis was one of the sweetest, kindest, most straightforward, and funniest people I had ever known. The moment Alice and I came to Mission of Love Full Gospel Church, Betty took to us. She always had something good, sarcastic, and funny to say, but she was always consistent and highly relatable to all the young people at the church.

The last Sunday in February, after church, she said to me, "I've been watching you. Are you working, or are you still laid off? I have an opportunity to hire a few people in my department."

I said, "I'm still laid off and searching, but yes, I am interested."

She began to explain that it was a consultant's position at the Chicago Public Schools Board of Education main office, but "If you get your foot in the door, it could turn into something permanent."

That was the quickest yes I had ever given for something I knew nothing about, but I trusted Betty. But more importantly, I trusted God for these next steps.

True to her word, she got me hired in March as a consultant in the Former Student Records department as a microfilm operator. I didn't have any benefits at that point, but the pay was good, and just like I prayed, I worked 8:30 a.m. to 4:30 p.m. Monday through Friday with weekends off.

The months went by, and working with Betty was pure joy. She ran a tight ship but allowed discretion for family and other minor life circumstances.

I came in early a few times and would catch her walking by herself, praying over the department, and I would inquire as to her purpose. I know you probably think it's self-explanatory, but I was in a continuous faith learning mode, and at that point in my life, I had not known of anyone walking around their job praying so earnestly. Sure, I had heard of someone praying softly at their desk or perhaps on a lunch break, but this seemed to be bolder with confidence. We talked for a little while before others arrived, and she explained that God's reality has to become our reality, as a foundation for every part of our life, including the workplace. The conversation was much more in depth than I write. But to make sure I keep things in context, what she meant was that she believed all things are possible with God and that He gave us authority to know Him and His way intimately. Therefore, the peace, joy, knowledge, and provision for home, work, and family can be accessed and spoken into existence through prayer.

She said, "The more you practice with sincerity, the more confident you become as He answers your prayer...He will always lead you right and never into ignorance."

She got there early, before her start time and other people, because we are not called to be a spectacle or distraction when we're supposed to be working. Betty went on to say that God had done so many wonderful things for her life and family because she learned how to trust Him. I digested a lot of what she taught, and because of her, I wanted to believe God would provide more for my family.

As the months went by, other members of our church got hired, and things were going well. Alice got a new and better job working out in Oak Brook for McDonald's Corporation headquarters. I was content and grateful, but I wanted a permanent position with the benefits that Betty had explained were so good. But the more I inquired, the less it seemed likely it would happen. All of the things I had learned about faith to that point seemed to be challenged.

It was January of 1994, and I still didn't have a permanent position. Not to mention, I got a call from Alice saying that the car had stopped on the highway while she was headed home. We had cell phones at that time. They were becoming popular and affordable, but the constant communication we have now was not the norm.

When she first called, she said, "I'm driving, and I periodically hear engine noise."

I said, "Stay where you are, and I'll be there."

She said, "I think I can meet you at home, but if something changes, I'll call back."

Not knowing information or having to depend on someone else for it was not comfortable for me, not to mention that I was super worried about my wife being in this position. She called back and explained that she heard a loud tapping noise, then loud clinking before the car just stopped and rolled to the side of the road. I would learn later that the oil pump gave up causing severe engine damage.

I quickly headed to her location. I'm not sure why circumstances that evening seemed to upset and bother me more than usual. But all I can remember is fusing to myself and saying to God, "How could you let this happen to my wife? And why don't I have a permanent position right now? You know they probably won't finance us for a car without me having a permanent job."

It wasn't that serious, and Alice was OK. But the idea of my wife on the side of the road broken-down was something I did not like, and I felt insulted that it happened to us.

A few minutes before I got to where Alice was I composed myself from my little temper tantrum and wiped a couple of tears. I could hear a small voice inside say, *"What are you doing? Your life is not as bad as you're making it out to be. And haven't you experienced favor in inopportune times before?"*

I got to where Alice was, and before I got out, I prayed that the circumstances would work out in our favor and that I would trust Him from now on, and not allow my emotions or fear to guide me or what I say. At that point, all I wanted to do was to assure my wife that everything was going to be all right.

I got out and began to check things out, and, sure enough, I could hear and see that her car was done. We got in the other car. Alice had that worried look on her face and asked, "What are we going to do? Because I work farther out, and we have to transport the children in the morning before we go to work."

I kept a brave face and said, "Let's go solve this problem tonight."

There was a car dealership not far off the highway that we were led to. As we pulled up, Alice said, "They may give us a hard time because you're not permanent."

I said, "Let's just go see and trust we'll meet someone who will work with us."

—⁂—

That evening, we were able to buy Alice a car with a small down payment and with me not having a permanent position. They gave us five hundred dollars for our broken-down trade-in, but the most favorable thing was, somehow that month, they received a lot of pre-driven factory demos that they wanted sold by month's end. The manager said they were easing some restrictions to move those cars, and thankfully this happened at the exact time that we needed a second vehicle.

Alice was excited that she had a really good car and no more worries, but I was so thankful to see her at peace. She got in the new car with a big smile and said, "Let's go get the kids." Never mind that only one of us had to go get the kids. We were excited and didn't care, so I drove my car following from behind.

While on the way, I remembered being happy but, for some reason, a little ashamed of myself for the way I reacted. But as usual, that voice came to me again and asked, "*Why are you feeling shame or regret for actions that you were able to overcome with knowledge and trust that I created you to walk in regardless of what you face?*" At that moment, it seemed as if the testimonies and experiences of my parents, people who had encouraged me, mixed with my own, flooded my heart with thanks. Immediately, and from that moment forward, I decided I would always believe that God's promises concerning my life, family, and health would guide my thoughts, mouth, and actions.

Convincing others that faith is innate to all of us is part of my passion. Once understood, its benefit is eye-opening to what we possessed all along. Our basis for reality can be influenced by the culture we live in and can impact the way we perceive what is real. One of the meanings for the word *reality* is "of or relating to practical or everyday concerns or activities." What are our everyday practices? What are we concerned about? And what do we allow ourselves to be active in from day to day?

It is quite possible to declare that our perception of things is the only truth and that other things are fraudulent or don't exist. I choose to believe we all were created with the same measure of faith or equal ability to believe. The question is how we continuously develop that measure.

As a child, what do we see and hear that become our practices? What do we relate to, care about, and struggle with? These cultural activities shape us, give us access to what we will believe, and then present us to the world and its circumstances.

The thing about faith that is so exciting is the possibility. If you can hear something different, say something different, and have an alternative outlook for your concerns based on different promises and hope, then your reality can change. Keep in mind that I am not suggesting that you not see things that are tangible since those things are born out of our ability.

Faith does not excuse us from good work or fruitful action. Quite the contrary, it supports an idea or a hope or an imagination coming to life or reality.

If you are reading this, I want to encourage you. Everything I just wrote is beneficial, but I have to tell you that this advice is awesome with God as the source reality. Your greatest distraction in life will be self. Every good thing in your life was what you were created for. Those negative, sometimes tragic things that have shown up periodically are temporary and a part of everyone's life, but I believe faith is always present, seeking to prepare and strengthen us for everyday circumstances in life. Whatever decision you make, I hope that you would at least consider a path that accentuates your God-given ability—that you practice receiving and displaying the highest level of God's peace and that that reality overwhelms you with all the success that you were created for.

Chapter 7

CHANGE

The following statement may sound ironic and is probably far from mind until we perceive something different is needed and that something has to give. We wrestle with the idea of people needing to act right or "the way I like," and if the circumstance would just see it my way, that would change my life. This often seems to be the perfect analysis and antidote for the modification of course needed. We, more than likely, haven't fully comprehended the depth of our outlook and view enough to realize, *this is my personal crossroad for change and new direction.* As I start to process, I have to ask is change really change if we replace one with another or shift from this to that? I do understand that we were taught to look up and reference words and their meanings in order to grasp the significance of a thing, but where is the true transformation attained?

I was done with making excuses, seeing what others were doing, being irritated for a circumstance, and allowing those things to dictate my attitude and actions. I was going to put the work in to be a better me regardless of what happened or didn't happen. They say that practice makes perfect, but that is probably one of the most incomplete statements that one could make. If I practice something incorrectly constantly, then I will more than likely become perfect at being incorrect and tragically share that with someone else. But if I learn to practice correctly, as perfectly as I can, then my growth to perfection is comprehended. I will admit up front, I had to remind myself constantly that change wasn't going to happen on its own, and my tendencies wouldn't be altered unless I actively engaged.

—⚬—

Over the next few months, I focused on being happy and grateful at home and on my job. I refocused myself when it came to communication in my household, and I tried to make myself more valuable at work by learning different things beyond what was required, even though I was a consultant.

In May of 1994, I had heard that there were positions opening up but didn't focus or put much energy toward them. I just figured; *if it is for me, then it will happen.* Then, all of a sudden, at the end of May just before the holiday, Betty, with a smile on her face called me to her desk and said, "You need to go up to see Paula on the sixth floor to sign some paperwork,"

I looked at her and said, "What kind of paperwork?"

She simply said, "Mr. Posegay, our manager, was able to open up a position in this department for you."

I smiled and stared.

She laughed and said, "Get going. This is not a joke."

On the way up, I was excited but didn't know what to expect. So I said to myself, "Don't say anything to Alice until you know everything is official."

After a background check and a drug test, I got the official letter for start date and benefits package. On June 13, 1994, I became a permanent employee with the Board of Education in the city of Chicago as a microfilm operator. That evening, I got home and told Alice about the good news. She was overjoyed, especially as I began to explain the benefits. Being able to transfer from her costly health insurance was the biggest blessing for us; it would mean more money into our household. As a personal victory, I was finally able to get back to carrying important weight in our home. I'm not referencing any male-ego stereotype because Alice and I were always in it together, for better or worse, and it never bothered me if she carried us when necessary. But I made a promise to myself and to her dad that I would take care of her. This may not register with everyone for different reasons, but I wanted to always keep my word. And so in my heart, there was always this sense of duty. Not to mention, as I continued to mature and change for the good, I realized I'm made for this.

Time went on, and the children were getting older and bigger, but the apartment refused to grow in size with them. I say that in jest, but the reality was that we needed more space and that changes were happening in our household whether we liked it or not. In 1997, appetites were growing, feet were larger, and one bathroom was being utilized constantly. I mentioned our financial situation before, and it was better, but Alice still loved to shop and probably could have been crowned the gold queen at that time in her life. I was always a stickler for paying bills on time and watching my credit and would always mention it to Alice in passing. She would say, "I got it." And I wouldn't worry.

The summer came, and getting a home for my family rested heavy on me. I spied a couple of homes in the south suburbs that listed for decent prices but were considered HUD homes, which means they were as is and needed work. I, however, did not do my homework and put the cart before the horse, so to speak. I found a private group that worked with HUD, who were realtors/brokers who let us look at the homes. We saw one that we liked and just decided to go for it, without making sure we knew the process or were financially sound enough to secure a mortgage.

I believe the realtors/brokers meant well, and I put blame squarely on my shoulders without hesitation. They explained the process to us and didn't try to hide anything from us, but I will say the process was not for new home buyers, especially if you are really green. They explained that you have to put a deposit of five hundred down on the property, and then you have thirty days to secure funding for property. Of course, we didn't secure funding and lost our five hundred dollars, mostly because we didn't qualify together. The other part was me not doing my homework for home or property ownership. The process I had dived into was for an investor or someone who understood quick closings; it was not for first-time home buyers. But again, you can never rely on someone else to make sure you know what you should know. We moved past the disappointment and decided that we were going to be better for it and never caught like that again.

—⁂—

As 1998 came in, Alice caught the "I want a house" bug, and I was so ready but didn't think she was serious because of her shopping habits and credit monitoring. We were really good at communicating at this point, and she would constantly bring it up, and I would say again, "We'll look when you really get serious." We got really good at saving money and planned on a vacation to Disney World for the kids. As we got close to the time to go to Florida, Alice mentioned the home again, but this time she talked about it in great detail and desire, and I was all ears because she was preaching to the choir. She had been working vigorously since the beginning of the year to pay off student loans and other little things that lingered from before we got married. I would watch and smile because I was glad to wait until I knew for sure we could do this together. We went on vacation and had a ball, not to mention we actually bought a timeshare while we were on vacation in Orlando. We figured the investment would be good for the family well into the future, and we got a really good deal.

We had transformed ourselves into keen observers when it came to any business, and so all that year, we spent time preparing ourselves for home ownership as well as the investments that we were making in our children. We wanted them to have every opportunity to grow and become all that God had created them to be. So the tuition and other paid activities were worthwhile to us. We had our eyes and heart open that year to take another shot, but my job started to crack down on their residential rules. If you owned outside of the city prior to a specific date, then you were exempt. But moving forward, you were required to live inside city limits. This didn't hinder us. It just changed our focus toward target areas in the city of Chicago. We kept saving money, and Alice kept working on her credit. She even started a consultant business for office support.

In 1999, we went on vacation again. Alice had been packing boxes here and there. She started to talk about what she wanted her kitchen to look like and even started to have the kids engage by faith.

She would say to them, "What do you want your room to look like?" And they would respond with all their desires. I saw transformation and was excited.

So after we talked, I said, "OK. After we come home from vacation, we will start the process."

Sure enough, that September we had dived in. But this time, we engaged with a highly recommended mortgage broker who had a lot of knowledge, which helped Alice and me to understand the industry she worked for. She made sure that we were educated in all the terms and made us aware of the questions to keep in mind when making this type of investment. We secured our mortgage and had a letter of credit funding, which let us know how much to spend and signaled that we were serious buyers.

We had been in Mrs. Crockett's building for a little over nine years, and after we secured mortgage funding, I made it a point to go and talk to her about our plans. She had been instrumental in my growth as a young man and father—with her support to my family well-being and her encouragement that I could do anything. She and her husband treated us like we were their children, and I was so grateful for that special day when she called us to offer the apartment in her building. Words could not express how she had helped change and shape the course of our life just by obeying the voice of God and changing our alternative path for the better in a matter of days. She was really happy for us and said, "You guys deserve it," and that we had also been a blessing to her as she was only months away from paying off her mortgage.

We engaged with Century 21 for house listings in an area not far from my parents, and we met a realtor named Ted. He was in his late seventies but was a really kind man who patiently worked with us. Over the month, we saw a few homes but nothing we could agree on. The kids were back in school, and the weather was also changing. Our families on both sides were important to us. Alice had the larger family, and many of them had moved to the south suburbs, just like us. We were used to being close to her parents and one of her sisters, but this move would change our proximity.

Over the years, Alice and I had grown so much. We had experienced different times and emotions that we believe prepared us for this time. Our church family, the involvement with ministry, and the disciplines we submitted to;

prepared us to be mature in change. This may not be everyone's thought, but we considered certain family ties, like other close families, and I knew Alice liked the convenience of being close to her parents. But we had a peace in knowing that because our location was changing, our responsibility and commitment to family would remain. Our families were praying with us that we would find that perfect home that we had in mind.

In November, Ted called and said he had a couple of homes he wanted us to see that evening after we got off work. It was late, dark, and of course the weather was cold, but we soldiered on to the first house. It was on a main, busy street. So no; we have children. But Ted asked if we could be courteous and keep the appointment, so we went in to look. It was a waste of time and caused us to miss the cutoff time for viewing the second home. But Ted called, and the owners said, "If you're not far, you can come." We were only five minutes away.

I need for you to imagine our hope, mental picture, and desire for what we wanted in a home. Alice kept saying, even before we started looking for a home, that she wanted a roomy kitchen, not large, that resembled my parents' kitchen. Tarail, our oldest who was now sixteen, wanted his room by himself in the basement. Marcus Jr. wanted his room to have football wallpaper, and Octavia just wanted a pink room. I was basic and thought about structural concerns. I simply wanted a brick home with a two-car garage but was also praying that the garage would also be brick.

We pulled up to the house. It was brick. We walked in, greeted the owners, then something changed. Alice and I looked at each other, and she grabbed my hand and smiled. We walked through the living room, which was a nice size. Then, all of a sudden, we were in the hallway and, looking to the right, there was a bedroom painted in pink, not far from the master bedroom. We then proceeded through the hallway into a kitchen that looked like my mom's kitchen. I thought Alice was going to explode. She said to the wife, "Oh my God, this resembles my mother-in-law's kitchen." As excited as we were, we looked to the left off the dining room, and there was a bedroom with football wallpaper on the wall. We were done and in love with the home, but God was not done transforming our thought into reality. We went down to the basement, and yes, it was completely finished with a bedroom. We didn't say too much out loud in excitement because we knew an offer would have to be placed, but there was more.

My direction and focus were shifted toward my family getting what they wanted and needed, but to my surprise as we went outside in the backyard; there was a brick two-car garage. This was real, and for me and Alice, that evening will never be forgotten. It altered the way we would see manifested faith forever. As you can imagine, we put in an offer, got an inspection, and in December 1999, we closed on our home.

I can imagine that if you look at a small part of your life, like me, you would notice the unique times that might have transformed, or at least aided in, the impact of a shift in direction. Those times distinguished what you were from what you became. These events, though they seem small, play the largest part in change of heart, attitude, perception, and even our outlook. It's no secret that you don't have to be a person of faith to have this experience, but I will reiterate that the core of understanding and a deeper sense of identity are wholly tied to faith. Whether or not you agree or choose a different path, I still say you deserve the best that life can offer.

Life's dips, curves, valleys, and peaks offer a huge range of emotions, thoughts, and perception, but they never deny us an opportunity. It may sound strange, but think about just a couple of the crossroads or decisions of your life that needed and depended on the very next thing that you would think, say, or put action to. An instant before you proceeded, an opportunity presented itself. It started to question the knowledge you had gained, stored, or would need. It rehearsed in a nanosecond any wisdom or logic that could potentially be of help in that critical moment. That choice marked itself in the history of your existence. Whether you were equipped or not, that decision made a difference and gave you all of its harvest.

I'm hoping to encourage, putting people ahead of this curve and ensuring that they know that, moving forward, we can monitor the choices that change and impact our lives. I've put a lot of thought into this, and as you know, I've made mistakes. I chose to let faith influence my life, and when I made positive and good choices, it was that change that truly transformed my destiny and took full advantage of opportunity.

There would be more to come in my life, and I am by no means trying to minimize what another person may face or the severity of that situation. I will say that the opposite of good and positive is bad and negative. If one were to choose the opposite, the only course or direction you could follow is a life of bad and negative results. Bad and negative decisions can cause separation in family, social, and work relationships. They blind you to the knowledge that can transform and make room for the opportunity that you deserve, not to mention the transformation would continue to reveal its harvest in time.

My life started to change. As I chose better, I could see better, and it didn't matter what was going on around me. I learned my choices had an impact on my children. Their joy, peace, and lack of fear started with me and Alice. Positive choice transformed me into a magnet for the knowledge and people designated for the seasons of my life that would prepare me for my opportunities. Without allowing and submitting to change, I might have been too bitter, angry, ornery, or even rebellious to see, comprehend, or receive the wisdoms, relationships, and the good things that were headed my way.

Chapter 8

DISTRESS AND PAIN WERE NEVER MY ENEMIES

The turn of the century had come. We were squarely in the year 2000—but no flying cars. We had settled into the new home, gotten a rhythm to our new routine, and begun to make plans for future projects. But even the best-laid plans are subject to life and its swift moving parts.

Alice's dad was a wonderful man with a high degree of integrity and honor. I would sit and talk with him, and I knew that what he said he meant from the heart, and he always had good intentions. Over the years, he had health challenges but never complained and always had a kind word to say. Alice and her brothers and sisters were always committed to their parents, and in the latter years, they had to help their dad more frequently. He and his wife had sixteen children, to which Alice was number fourteen. They would spend a lot of time going back and forth to help their mom make sure that he was comfortable and had whatever he needed. Like me, he was a die-hard Cubs fan, and whenever

I'd go by, if there was a game on, he was watching. He would say, "One of these days, Marc, we are going to go to Wrigley Field and watch the game."

I would smile and say, "You got it."

He and I never made it to the park. And in 2000, he passed away.

We had experienced loss of friends, loved ones, and extended family, but nothing prepares you for loss of immediate family—brothers, sisters, and parents.

I had come to love Alice's parents like my own and felt the impact of his passing. But having to experience Alice going through the grief process for the first man she had known brought a feeling of helplessness that I can still feel today. We both were used to having fathers and mothers in our lives, with access to them within minutes since they all lived in the Chicago and surrounding areas. To see their faces and hear their voices was as normal to us as our heartbeat.

Alice took her dad's transition really hard, but she had to balance her grief, like her brothers and sisters, to maintain a level of strength for her mom. I was a problem solver, but this was something that we could only comprehend in time. I could only comfort her tears, which would come without warning at any time of the day. Simply being there or letting her have space seemed like the only thing I could do. As people of faith, we believe in eternal life after transitioning from this life, but this process was so personal. If we ever had a question as whether the grief process is a real thing to contend with, Alice and I can wholeheartedly say yes.

I want to make sure I explain the context of our grief process because Alice didn't lose contact with reality. She knew and accepted that her dad was no longer here. Alice, her mom, and her brothers and sisters all carried on. But grief is the longing to have just one more conversation, smile, hug, sound of voice, and flood of memories that seem as if they are happening at that very moment, regardless of how long ago they were. Her dad and his legacy were imprinted on her very existence. There was no how-to manual for coping with him not being here physically, as many others in similar circumstances can relate to. And like so many who face this part of life understand his passing and absence of physical presence would take time to get used to.

A couple of years passed, and life, as it does, kept moving as it did with our children. They were older now. We had our oldest who had graduated from high school, one getting ready for high school, and our baby girl trying to become a preteen. Like many, but not everyone, we had our days and a time of stress with our children, and each one was different. I know a few people can relate when I say that your first child can make you into a pro, depending on the depth of training you endure to get them from one goal to the next. While each personality and issue was different, we committed to putting in the same level of concern and desire for them to always come out on top. We really believed that their potential was based on what God created them for, and we never surrendered to any amount of dismay that tried to influence the heart.

After Tarail graduated, he would face a few battles that were daunting, especially for him personally. He was smart and comprehended most things in life, including school. But like some, he was drawn to other paths. He would later become better and learn how to navigate life with more urgency. Marcus Jr. had his struggles academically, but with a lot of tutoring, he grew into a bright young man. And like his brother, he is a formidable piano player and musician. Octavia was my little princess who was getting older too fast. She was daddy's little girl for a while, but as she got older, she would cling to her mom and often whisper what she didn't want me to know. (You know lady stuff.)

Our children were what we lived for, and for any situation they came upon, we were willing to make it a part of our life and absorb some of the impact, to a point. We had given them the best start that we knew how and resolved that we would always be a part of their lives as they continued to mature. Raising children can be challenging yet you would give your life for them. Unforeseen issues can happen that make you second guess yourself, and though they take time and consume levels of care, you make room and keep going.

It is the situation that you don't see coming until it is right in your face that shakes your life. Alice's sister Margaret (we called her Mickey) started to become ill, and we would find out later that she had colon cancer. She was sweet, serious, and funny, all at the same time. Margaret was very dependable and was always ready to say yes. She was a sister who you could lean on: a babysitter for just about all of her nieces and nephews and a constant rock for her parents.

Margaret was also married. Her husband's name was Van. He was a really good guy who worked at the Board of Education with me for a time, and he would brag constantly on the job about how much he loved his wife. As she progressed, we all started to pay close attention, especially their sister Deloris. They were really close and often inseparable. She would make sure of doctors' visits, medications, and just about anything that Van and Margaret needed for support. After a few complications and a valiant battle, Margaret transitioned from this life. This was a sting that you never get used to. It never matters that you have experienced the passing of a close and immediate loved one. When it happens, it is unwanted and heart-wrenching, like nothing you want to feel. I cried, but Alice cried many nights, and the only thing I could do was just be there. Death is the thing you never want to talk about, think on and defiantly be a part of, but when it comes it leaves its impression on those that remain by reminding us that we are mortal.

After a few months, Alice and her sisters began to have discussions about Margaret's battle and began to educate themselves on colon health. They pledged to each other, in commemoration of Margaret, to go and get screenings every year.

—∿—

Distress and pain can leave their marks; the hope is that they are as brief as possible and that their season is temporary. Sometimes it's easy to feel like you're experiencing loss in an unrealistic pattern. But the truth is life has always been swift, and time with our love ones should be cherished and not wasted.

In December of 2003, we saw life beginning. We welcomed our first grandchild into this world. Our son Tarail fathered his first child, a little boy named Tarail Jr. TJ, as we called him, had no idea that he was about to be spoiled by his grandmother. It was a welcome time and much needed focus on joyous things.

In 2004, we started to plan for Alice's family reunion, to be held in California. Her sister Gloria and Gloria's husband David were the hosts and communicated exciting plans for all to enjoy. We decided that we would take TJ with us on the airplane, even though I felt like he was still young. The new Grandma Alice could not help herself.

Leading up to June, we heard that their oldest brother, Joe, who lived in Las Vegas with his family, would meet us at the reunion. Alice had mentioned that he was a little under the weather but that he was excited that he would be seeing everyone. Unfortunately, a week before he could see anyone, his wife called and said he had passed. A few days later, the time came to leave for the reunion. Though hearts were heavy, we proceeded, in hopes that as we were there, we would celebrate his life.

Traveling had its challenges. To add to stress, TJ had a cold. He was a little cranky but manageable. The three-hour flight seemed like an eternity since keeping him busy and calm was the entire focus. We finally got ready to land in California, and, of course, TJ fell asleep. But this was fine since it gave us a chance to get to the hotel and get settled in. Seeing everyone was a wonderful feeling and just what this family needed at that moment in time. We spent a couple of days socializing and trying to comfort one another knowing that we weren't there just for a reunion but to also honor Joe.

While we were all together, we got a call from Joe's wife concerning his memorial plans. We quickly rallied together as Las Vegas was only about seven hours away. We all made it there safely to be with Joe's family, and to share in the memorial service. After spending the day in Las Vegas we made it back to California to wrap things up with family and say our goodbyes. We would all make our way back to our separate homes. But in some ways, it felt like we did get a chance to be with Joe. The memories that were relived between family members gave life to his legacy and made me feel like I had known him for a lifetime.

A couple of years passed, and we had our last two children in high school. This was also the beginning of the housing market crash and its effects on the stock market. This beat up our home value, especially since we had taken equity out to do some projects. Not to mention, Alice opened a clothing store in Evergreen Plaza. She had worked hard, gotten her business plan settled, and negotiated a really good deal with the mall management. It was just a terrible time to have a startup business—in the middle of a recession that would progressively get worse. It was bleaker than we thought. We tried to keep going, and we sunk a lot of money into the venture along with other personal investments. Alice was persistent, and it was stressful for a time, but we kept going.

My parents took a really big blow to their retirement savings also. Like many, they lost a large sum of money that they would not recover. As I said, we all kept going, but I think it weighed on my dad more heavily than he let on. In 2008, he suffered a mild heart attack. He tried to calm everyone by saying it just happened randomly, but I knew in my heart that he was a little sad for what he had spent years of his life earning, now partially vanished. My parents were resilient and saw it as a temporary setback, for me and Alice, after some restructuring of debt, we were able to move on from the recession and absorb its lingering effects.

In 2010, all seemed to be going well. Octavia was our last child in high school, and it was her senior year. I was joyful and even got my chest sticking out thinking about her graduation, prom, and getting her off to college. It was a good season for me and Alice. We were able to be a blessing to a lot of people, including being able to gift someone with one of our vehicles.

I was off work for a minor holiday, but Alice had to work, so I drove her. But on the way, she was quiet. Then, all of a sudden, she said, "I've got something to tell you." She proceeded to utter words that I will never forget. She said, "Octavia is pregnant." It felt like someone put their foot through the windshield and kicked me in the chest. She started crying, and I couldn't say anything.

I think I stayed quiet for two weeks before I could say anything. I wasn't in pain, but pain might have been better at that point. A lot of people tried to offer words of encouragement by saying things like "All you can do now is be a father and be supportive." Be a father! And be supportive!

What was I doing all these other years? We got past it, and Octavia graduated on time. In August of that year, she gave birth to a little boy and named him Ryan Jr. We love to call him RJ. He came into my life and became my little man.

That same year, Alice's Brother Greg—who was a great musician and, over the years, was as close as any brother I had could be—passed away with respiratory complications. Alice and I both felt the impact of Greg's passing and spent a lot of time praying for God's comfort over the family. Greg was a huge part of the gospel community of musicians and choirs with several recorded songs. I can still hear his voice when I think about him, and Alice sometimes cries when thinking of him. But we kept going because Alice and her sisters and brothers had to focus on their mom.

In 2011, Alice's mom's dementia started to escalate while dealing with other health issues. She was strong-willed and could still quote scriptures even if names slipped her mind. She lived with Alice's older sister Georgia. They all would take turns in the care of their mom by going to Georgia's home in shifts.

Georgia took their mom to Oklahoma to visit with another sister, Annie, and her husband George. George and Annie would come to reunions to be with family and randomly pop up to check on their mom, but this time they wanted to spend time and cater to Georgia Lee and mom in their hometown. They were out on the town one evening having a wonderful time when suddenly their mom lost consciousness and transitioned that evening. We were stung again as family, but with the help and leadership of their older brother George we endured the pain of missing two parents and put their mom to rest beside her husband, their father.

Alice and all of her brothers and sisters are people of faith, the strength that they displayed in spite of their brother passing and then their mother in such a short span of time is something that I will always admire. I believe that strength came from their mother; she was a praying woman and believed in her family being close and praying together. I grew to love her like my own mom and will forever be grateful that she called me son and gave life to my wife.

Alice and I were blessed as grandparents and very fortunate that our grandchildren had met great-grandparents on both sides. I still had both parents and my grandmother on my mom's side in my life, or I should say *our* life. Alice took to my parents and my grandmother like her own. They felt the same way about Alice without hesitation. In 2012, my dad started experiencing complications with blood clots. He was really stubborn and hated taking the medications, and whenever the doctor would say something, he had a different opinion. Both my parents were mobile and could still drive so they didn't need us to hover over them. It didn't stop us from going by just about every day to check on them since Alice and I weren't far away.

One evening, I got a call from my mom saying she was taking dad to the emergency room because he was having trouble walking. I rushed over, and, of course, he didn't want to go. But I persisted, and he finally said OK. We got him there, and they checked him in and said there were more clots in his lungs. I called my brothers and sister to let them know what was going on and mentioned that the doctors were very concerned. We were so used to my dad being this strong man who seemed invincible that we never thought any other way.

A day later, while he was still admitted, complications arose, and they had to revive him. This didn't seem like any reality we had known, I was used to having two healthy parents. As the doctors began to explain that we almost lost him, we understood but believed that he would come through and that we should be there to help him do what was necessary to stay with us.

A couple of days passed, and he was able to move out of the ICU to a regular room. We were grateful and optimistic, but the doctors didn't seem to be all that positive. They kept reminding my mother that he was still very sick. But to look at my dad, you would believe that he was coming back around. He spent a few more days and didn't seem better or worse, so we continued praying and believing that he would turn around.

One evening, I sat with him, and we watched the Chicago Bulls play. After the game he looked at me and said, "Marcus, you go home and get some rest. And make sure you see after your mother."

I said, "OK, dad. You know I'll do that."

He said again, "OK, go ahead. I'll be OK."

I said, "I love you. Have a good night. I'll see you tomorrow."

That morning, at about 7:00 a.m., my mom and I both got calls saying my dad was having a bad morning and that we should get there as soon as possible. I hurried to pick up my mom and rushed to the hospital, but by the time we got there, my dad had passed. My brothers and sister arrived, and we dealt with the anguish of his passing. But I wanted to remain strong for my mother.

After a few hospital details, my family prayed together. And as we walked out, I stood next to my mom, and she grabbed my arm. We began to walk, and she started to talk about how she'll miss him.

I said, "Don't worry. He told me to take care of you, and I promised I would."

At that moment, I couldn't walk, and tears started to flow uncontrollably. She grabbed me, along with my other family, and said, "I know, but we'll take care of each other."

Time passed, and we were stronger, wiser, and truly grateful on both sides of our families. We enjoyed watching our families expand and become fruitful in every sense of the word. Alice also fulfilled part of the promise we made to each other when we were young by completing her bachelor's degree in business. I was so proud and gladly wanted to make sure that she was first to do what we knew would take time and some sacrifice.

We, like everyone else, would make plans for our future but understood that we were older. We wanted to make the last years of our careers really work to put us in a position of freedom after retirement. We were mature and had grown over the years to understanding that God was our source. I wake up every morning with a grateful heart and love to say, "Thank you."

We also understood that we were not exempt from circumstances that can happen to anyone. January 2015 was here, and Alice had been hearing rumors of downsizing within her company. No one had a lot of details, but we wouldn't have to wait long as that same month Alice got laid off. We absorbed the impact and committed to making certain adjustments while she took a well-deserved break before diving back into the market. After all, I still had my job, and our health benefits were with me. The year passed, and all seemed to be stable. And more importantly, our household had peace.

January 2016 was here, and my job started to declare unstable times, but for some reason, I just refused to give it energy. At the end of the month, on a Friday, we were summoned to the main office location to find out our fate. I arrived; noticing that many had tears in their eyes for fear that it would be their last day. But I had a peace and made up my mind: whatever the outcome, I would keep going. It seemed like the longest morning I had experienced in a long time, but just before noon, I went in for my meeting. I sat down, and, of course, the person sitting across from me seemed to stumble with remorse and finally said, "I'm so sorry, but you are being laid off."

It had been a long time since I heard those words, but this time they didn't have the sting that was to be expected. At that moment, all I could do was think about how in the last twenty-two years I had been blessed to take care of my family, raise my children, and not have an ounce of regret or anger toward anyone. I said a few "see you later" goodbyes to my colleagues and proceeded to call Alice. But like me, she said, "We'll be OK," and reminded me that we had a birthday dinner to go to.

I wasn't thrilled nor was I upset that I didn't have a job anymore. And for a split second, I did think about our health benefits and a few details for our household, like many who face this path. Before dinner that evening I took a shower to wash away the events of the day, with my head under the water and for about sixty seconds, I thought about what the human resource person said in trying to ease the conversation. She said, "I know this is a difficult day, and if I could trade places with you, I would." I knew she meant well and was at a loss for words in having to repeat the task to others, but at that moment, I told myself I should have taken her up on her offer to see if she meant it. But that same inner peace came over me again and said, "Stop it. She didn't mean harm, and you have seen this before. But this time you can hear me."

Over the coming weeks, I would tell my story and would always give God credit for my life. One particular evening, after about a month, we went to dinner with my brother-in-law Michael and Alice's sister Laura. While at dinner, Michael asked, "What are you going to do now?"I smiled and said, "God is my source, and I'm going to keep going on to the next thing."

The last sixteen years brought the stress and pain of sickness, grief from the passing of loved ones and friends, struggles within our family, and impacts from social and economic challenges. I only mention parts in brief detail to hopefully relate to some who might have seen these times and circumstances. Nonetheless, I can not only imagine but also fully comprehend that these times can be overwhelming and, for many, a constant source of torment. The grief alone is enough to keep you in a mental loop that keeps replaying the loss and absence of those we held so dear.

As loud as the circumstances have been, I was prepared and not afraid to listen. If they had anything else to say to me, now was the time to speak up. As these seasons in my life started to talk, I heard the voices of my passed loved ones say, "You never lost me. We will always be connected by the love we share, which will never cease. No one can ever erase the conversations, the words we spoke, the secrets we shared, the goofy times, the sad times, the disagreements, the hugs, and, yes, even my transition. You don't just know me; I'm a part of you for eternity."

When I look at my children and think about the few things that I mentioned, I have to remind myself that it wasn't just what I was experiencing, but they too had an experience of their own. Having me and Alice as parents help prepare them, just like my parents prepared me, for the paths they would choose, even if their scenery was always going to be different than mine. Our seasons can and will come in many variations of pain, loss, and distress. Even if you feel like you are at your lowest, you are still here and have so much more to give. First, pick your head up and receive the love of God that will never fade. Then, be encouraged and know that these circumstances are not there to destroy you. They come with time's swiftness. They leave seeds that grow in us with wisdom, patience, courage, and, best of all, signs that point us to the future. They also remind us that, like our ancestors, as you move forward in grace, you carry a legacy of hope, unending inner strength, and knowledge that you will be OK.

Chapter 9

TIRED OF DREAMING; GET TO WORK

How do we let so much time go by without harvesting the thoughts and ideas that are rehearsed in the processes of our minds? Or how do we make manifest those idealistic yet fantastic images of ourselves from daydreams? My parents would say, "You can be anything that you set your heart to." But I don't think I truly ever tested the theory.

Over the years, many thoughts and great ideas have come, and the images that play over and over in my mind have wonderful intentions but often never get introduced to passion. When you're a child, thoughts of being great, doing something impactful, or anything your imagination could come up with seem to fade the older you become. They turn into daydreams or reminders of how much time you let pass if the corresponding actions have not been implemented or at least attempted. Most of us probably do a good job of admitting how we let certain hopes and dreams get away. But do we sit and think about why we moved away or placed them on hold so quickly, and in some cases indefinitely?

The will to put energy and motion toward something—to shift a dream to a concept, then that concept to a work pattern—are familiar notions that have stayed on my mind. I was surrounded by encouragement from high school to college, from my parents, my wife, peers, colleagues, church, books, DVDs, and seminars. Most of us don't make excuses. We try to rationalize why the challenge that came or the next opportunity coming is the reason we haven't poured ourselves into the very work that others have linked to our potential. If one or two years pass, we say to ourselves, "I need to work on my idea." We may even attempt to move in the direction of research for starting, but something takes us away. I have even been bold enough to take time off, do research, and then talk myself out of the next steps that require more effort than I was willing to give.

I have watched people who have poured themselves into their hopes and dreams then spent an equal amount of time watching them reap the benefits of persistence and passion. And while happy for these individuals, I'm left tormenting myself for the amount of time I have let parish. It's easy to say that I've had other responsibilities. But if I tell the truth, I'd have to admit that all the times I kept waiting for better timing or holding up my caution flag, while saying it was not logically safe to invest, were a strategy to nowhere. I have seen my children grow into adults and have children of their own, and I have watched and been proud to see my wife excel without hesitation. My family is my passion, and to see them flourish is an answer to my prayers. Yet there is still more, deep inside, with a voice calling out to my passion that it's time.

If self-reflection fulfills its purpose, it will bring clarity in its purist form. And for me, its truth is me starting to see that I am the one who put limits on my capacity. I finally understand that I have allowed opportunity to walk by while I say, "I'll catch you later." I can't speak for anyone else, but for me, "later" has created a backlog of untapped dreams and is occupying the space and atmosphere of my resolve and potential success.

Keep in mind that God's favor has been on my side, and my household has never suffered. My personal growth and life have been orchestrated by God, from the seeming impossible to possible, and He continues to be faithful. But somewhere along the line, I forgot to allow the same energy and authority to pour out of me for business ideas, investment ambition, and ministry goals. I understand that your goals, ideas, and dreams are more than likely different from mine, but hopefully, like me, you still believe. Even if your household structure, perception of life, cultural knowledge, or life experiences that have you on other paths are not the same, there is common ground.

We all want to succeed, and we have varying thoughts of what that looks like. For me, the focus is not money. But if it is for you, there is nothing wrong with that. Just keep in mind that those rewards generally take care of themselves in time. There may even be a scenario that I haven't accounted for nor have insight to you personally, and yet it won't diminish my hope for our journeys. In either case, we have all carried some type of dream. But the one thing that I am sure of and believe in my heart is that we were never meant to carry any form of our potential to the grave.

I thought to myself, "You should write a book. You have a little time on your hands since the workforce kicked you out." I'm joking, but I do have the time. But what would I say, or who would read what I had to say? I had so many thoughts, and I have always been a dreamer at heart but yielded to analytical and practical measures for most of my life. But things are about to change. The dream of writing this book has been with me for years. All of the things that I have experienced and hoped to accomplish were speaking to me loud and clear. This was more urgent to me than a passing idea or a suggestion to try my hand. I'm not even claiming to be a writer, but I do know that nothing will stop me from writing this book about parts of my life to help and encourage someone else in similar paths. For me, this is only the start of the many things I hope to accomplish in the coming future.

Our dreams give us a unique insight into the authority of our potential, and they plant a seed of possibility in each of us as we witness ourselves doing that very thing in an alternate reality of our being. When we try to reason that what we dream is not real, it doesn't change the fact that it is possible. Dreams that confirm our creative destiny, hopeful well-being, inner beauty, and every great thing that impacts the universe in a positive way are what we should aim for. It may seem as if so much time has passed and that some of the things that you would even consider entertaining from your dreams may be an overwhelming task, but remember you were made for this.

The first thing that we are going to do is write down what we saw ourselves doing or accomplishing, then we are going to read and say it out into the atmosphere. This may be an unusual experience for you, but it can be a practical start to the thing you desire most. By writing the thing down, you have a reference point that can be arranged in an order of wisdom. By reading out loud the thoughts and plans of your dream reality, you are giving them access to a pathway called hearing, which you are familiar with in terms of how you receive and implement action on a daily basis. Your dreams can become reality. If we write something by our hand, it leaves an impression. If we say the words, it becomes a habit. If we develop a habit, it brings hope. And hope seeks a path.

I'm finding out that this is not the hardest thing I've ever thought to do, and as a matter of fact, I'm finding out that the passion that I ignored all these years only wanted me to go with it while it did all the work. Passion and our dreams are best friends. They talk to each other constantly about you and me. They tell each other that this is what they were made for, and they gently work from the inside, away from other influences, hoping to be heard and provide help for what has always been possible.

Our capacity is so much greater than what we have gotten used to, and after today, I'm hoping that a spark ignites that causes a stir. There is so much that needs to be poured from you and me so that we can eliminate that dream backlog, and only you know what's calling you with passion. For me, my calling includes writing this book and the other ministry goals that I've dreamed about are being implemented, and after this book I've got another one burning on the inside of me. Your dreams and passion are waiting on you to give them permission by taking those first two steps. I believe with everything in me that as soon as you say yes, time will cheer you on as you move into the spaces that only you were designed for.

Chapter 10

SUCCESS AND BENEFITS ON THE INSIDE OF ME

O ver time, we are measured by many in different ways, and I believe they are always well intended. This is especially true when areas of success are touted or shown and when the benefits of that success are displayed and granted. We are taught from a young age that there is a scale and that you want it to tip toward you constantly. Subliminal messages signaled by our culture, as to what winning and accomplishing means or what incentives and gains should look like, are planted in our minds. And again, coming out on top is a positive message but doesn't completely reveal the perfect balance that gives understanding of that scale.

I often wondered about this accounting of my life, but I didn't take the time to explore or understand it until enough circumstances and events caused me to look for myself. Like many other people, I had a picture in my mind of what I thought success should look like given to me by my parents and others who I respected. They also helped me know what to look for in the area of benefits and the worth they beheld when finally attained. I am grateful for their wisdom and am not throwing it away, but I missed something or didn't give complete consideration to perfectly apply reason to their words. Words matter and seek to relay an idea for the thing that is intended. I could comprehend them, but true aim and a truth didn't appear until I finally gave way to an internal purpose of words that I had heard so many times. Life wasn't trying to deceive me; it was patiently communicating to me with levels of information in increasing tones as I matured. Growing in faith has taught me to listen more, and with it, a new level of discovery passion, working in me has brought light to something that I knew but didn't fully understand until now.

The guides and influences of our lives, regardless of how they are attained, train, culture, and prepare us for the expected narrative of success. Their forms and timings are assumed and planned but most certainly are subject to individual choice, desire, and will. This information is readily available but not comprehended in a way that helps us personally understand the responsibility of understanding true success or decide how our benefits present to us.

When I was young, I could grasp the idea of success and the favor one received from that success when I competed in academics, sports, or other performance-oriented milestones. Those things taught me to pursue, persist, and be confident. This type of training prepares you for a world that promotes this mindset and challenges all to play by these rules. That was the beginning of my path to what I believed a successful outcome should look like and how accomplished I felt once the reward came. This is a good thing as long as perspective